The San Francisco Earthquake of 1906

The San Francisco Earthquake of 1906

Lisa A. Chippendale

CHELSEA HOUSE PUBLISHERS
Philadelphia

Frontispiece: The massive earthquake that rocked
San Francisco, California, in 1906 initiated one of
the greatest disasters of the 20th century.

CHELSEA HOUSE PUBLISHERS

Production Manager Pamela Loos
Art Director Sara Davis
Director of Photography Judy L. Hasday
Managing Editor James D. Gallagher
Senior Production Editor J. Christopher Higgins

Staff for THE SAN FRANCISCO EARTHQUAKE OF 1906

Senior Editor LeeAnne Gelletly
Associate Art Director Takeshi Takahashi
Designer Keith Trego
Picture Researcher Patricia Burns
Cover Designer Keith Trego

First Printing

1 3 5 7 9 8 6 4 2

The Chelsea House World Wide Web address is
http://www.chelseahouse.com

Library of Congress Cataloging-in-Publication Data

Chippendale, Lisa A.
The San Francisco earthquake of 1906 : great disasters / Lisa
A. Chippendale.
  p. cm. — (Great disasters: reforms and ramifications)
Includes bibliographical references and index.

ISBN 0-7910-5270-2

1. Earthquakes—California—San Francisco—History—
20th century—Juvenile literature. 2. Fires—California—San
Francisco—History—20th century—Juvenile literature.
3. San Francisco (Calif.)—History—20th century—Juvenile
literature. 4. Earthquake prediction—Juvenile literature.
[1. Earthquakes—California—San Francisco. 2. San
Francisco (Calif.)—History—20th century. 3. Earthquake
prediction.] I. Title. II. Series.
F869.S357 C47 2000
979.4'61—dc21   00-031256

Contents

GREAT DISASTERS
REFORMS and RAMIFICATIONS

Jill McCaffrey
National Chairman
Armed Forces Emergency Services
American Red Cross

Introduction

isasters have always been a source of fascination and awe. Tales of a great flood that nearly wipes out all life are among humanity's oldest recorded stories, dating at least from the second millennium B.C., and they appear in cultures from the Middle East to the Arctic Circle to the southernmost tip of South America and the islands of Polynesia. Typically gods are at the center of these ancient disaster tales—which is perhaps not too surprising, given the fact that the tales originated during a time when human beings were at the mercy of natural forces they did not understand.

To a great extent, we still are at the mercy of nature, as anyone who reads the newspapers or watches nightly news broadcasts can attest.

Hurricanes, earthquakes, tornados, wildfires, and floods continue to exact a heavy toll in suffering and death, despite our considerable knowledge of the workings of the physical world. If science has offered only limited protection from the consequences of natural disasters, it has in no way diminished our fascination with them. Perhaps that's because the scale and power of natural disasters force us as individuals to confront our relatively insignificant place in the physical world and remind us of the fragility and transience of our lives. Perhaps it's because we can imagine ourselves in the midst of dire circumstances and wonder how we would respond. Perhaps it's because disasters seem to bring out the best and worst instincts of humanity: altruism and selfishness, courage and cowardice, generosity and greed.

As one of the national chairmen of the American Red Cross, a humanitarian organization that provides relief for victims of disasters, I have had the privilege of seeing some of humanity's best instincts. I have witnessed communities pulling together in the face of trauma; I have seen thousands of people answer the call to help total strangers in their time of need.

Of course, helping victims after a tragedy is not the only way, or even the best way, to deal with disaster. In many cases planning and preparation can minimize damage and loss of life—or even avoid a disaster entirely. For, as history repeatedly shows, many disasters are caused not by nature but by human folly, shortsightedness, and unethical conduct. For example, when a land developer wanted to create a lake for his exclusive resort club in Pennsylvania's Allegheny Mountains in 1880, he ignored expert warnings and cut corners in reconstructing an earthen dam. On May 31, 1889, the dam gave way, unleashing 20 million tons of water on the towns below. The Johnstown Flood, the deadliest in American history, claimed more than 2,200 lives. Greed and negligence would figure prominently in the Triangle Shirtwaist Company fire in 1911. Deplorable conditions in the garment sweatshop, along with a failure to give any thought to the safety of workers, led to the tragic deaths of 146 persons. Technology outstripped wisdom only a year later, when the designers of the luxury liner *Titanic* smugly declared their state-of-the-art ship "unsinkable," seeing no need to provide lifeboat capacity for everyone onboard. On the night of April 14, 1912, more than 1,500 passengers and crew paid for this hubris with their lives after the ship collided with an iceberg and sank. But human catastrophes aren't always the unforeseen consequences of carelessness or folly. In the 1940s the leaders of Nazi Germany purposefully and systematically set out to exterminate all Jews, along with Gypsies, homosexuals, the mentally ill, and other so-called undesirables. More recently terrorists have targeted random members of society, blowing up airplanes and buildings in an effort to advance their political agendas.

The books in the GREAT DISASTERS: REFORMS AND RAMIFICATIONS series examine these and other famous disasters, natural and human made. They explain the causes of the disasters, describe in detail how events unfolded, and paint vivid portraits of the people caught up in dangerous circumstances. But these books are more than just accounts of what happened to whom and why. For they place the disasters in historical perspective, showing how people's attitudes and actions changed and detailing the steps society took in the wake of each calamity. And in the end, the most important lesson we can learn from any disaster—as well as the most fitting tribute to those who suffered and died—is how to avoid a repeat in the future.

A Deep, Terrible Rumble

The San Francisco earthquake of 1906 caused extensive damage throughout the city. The first tremor struck without warning, heaving streets, twisting girders, collapsing walls and buildings, and hurling broken glass, bricks, and rubble into the streets.

A t 5:00 A.M. on Wednesday, April 18, 1906, most citizens of the prosperous port city of San Francisco, California, were quietly asleep. Only those who had to work early or who had stayed up late carousing in its many disreputable establishments were awake.

Police sergeant Jesse Cook was on duty at the produce market, located north of Market Street, the city's main thoroughfare, and a few blocks from the San Francisco Bay waterfront. In the early morning hours he watched market workers busily unloading produce from horse-drawn wagons in preparation for the business day. Sergeant Cook noticed that the cart horses seemed skittish, frequently neighing and nervously pulling at their reins. Their unusual behavior was his only warning that the worst earthquake in San Francisco's history was about to strike.

11

At 5:12 A.M. Cook heard "a deep rumble, deep and terrible, and then I could see [the earthquake] actually coming up Washington Street. The whole street was undulating. It was as if the waves of the ocean were coming towards me, billowing as they came." The shock tossed him helplessly off his feet as the buildings surrounding the area collapsed, crushing men and horses in an onslaught of bricks.

About 14 blocks away Fred Hewitt, a reporter for the *San Francisco Examiner,* had just stopped to speak with two policemen standing outside City Hall, at the corner of Golden Gate Avenue and Larkin Street. Only 10 years old, the $6 million building was topped by a grand, high dome that seemed to symbolize the prosperity and success of the booming city's inhabitants.

The immense tremor struck with fury. Later, Hewitt described what happened:

> It is impossible to judge the length of that shock. To me it seemed an eternity. I was thrown prone on my back and the pavement pulsated like a living thing. Around me the huge buildings, looming up more terrible because of the queer dance they were performing, wobbled and veered. Crash following crash resounded on all sides. . . . [Frightened] horses dashed headlong into ruins as they raced away in their abject fear.
>
> Then there was a lull. The most terrible was yet to come.

Hewitt managed to stagger to his feet during the next 10 seconds of calm. Then the earthquake continued with renewed vigor. The second shock was even longer and more severe than the first:

> The street beds heaved in frightful fashion. . . . [T]he old Supreme Court building danced a frivolous dance

and then tumbled into the street. . . . One lone line of frame buildings tottered a moment and then just as a score or more of terror-stricken, white-shirted humanity [managed] to reach the open, it laid [the buildings] flat. . . . The cries of those who must have perished reached my ears, and I hope that never again this side of the grave will I hear such signals of agony.

Finally the violent shaking, which had lasted from 45 to 60 seconds, ceased. The rumbling, groaning, clanging, and crashing abruptly turned to silence, punctuated only by the intermittent thuds of falling bricks and the screams and groans of the injured and trapped.

Even the grand City Hall, located at the intersection of McAllister Street and Van Ness Avenue, was not exempt from the power of the quake, which tore off ornate masonry and brickwork, leaving only the structure's steel birdcage-like tower intact.

In the turmoil immediately following the earthquake, residents grabbed loved ones and their most valuable possessions, then rushed for the safety of open areas. Aftershocks would continue to terrorize San Francisco's citizens, who sought refuge in city streets and parks.

Hewitt looked over at City Hall, which was obscured by a huge cloud of falling dirt and debris. He waited for the dust to settle, certain that the great building must have sustained serious damage. After a few minutes he could see that the great steel-framed dome of City Hall still stood, but it had been sheared of most of its masonry: "The dome appeared like a huge bird cage against the morning dawn. The upper works of the entire building laid . . . in the street below." The wrecked dome of City Hall could be seen throughout the stricken city. It was a grim signal that a disaster of epic proportions had just devastated San Francisco.

Frightened survivors poured into the rubble-strewn streets. Hewitt commented on their general panic, witnessed as he made his way from the City Hall area to his home:

Herds of huddled creatures, attired in next to nothing, occupied the center of the streets. Each and every person I saw was temporarily insane. Laughing idiots commented on the fun they were having. Terror marked their faces. . . . No one knew which way to turn, when on all sides of them destruction stared them in the very eye. A number of slight tremors followed the first. . . . As each came . . . terror stamped its mark in every brow.

Another early riser who was also outside when the temblor struck was Thomas Jefferson Chase. He later described what he saw while walking to his job at the Ferry Building, which was located at the foot of Market Street, on the bay:

I heard a low distant rumble. It was coming from the west, louder and louder. I stopped and listened. Then it hit.

Power and trolley lines snapped like threads. The ends of the power lines dropped to the pavement not 10 feet from where I stood, writhing and hissing like reptiles. Brick and glass showered about me.

Buildings along First Street from Howard to Market crumbled like card houses. One was brick. Not a soul escaped. Clouds of that obliterated the scene of destruction. The dust hung low over the rubble in the street.

As this shock stopped I crossed over to the east side of the street. . . . As soon as I reached the curb a second shock hit. This was harder than the first. I was thrown flat and the cobblestones danced like corn in a popper. More brick and glass showered down on the sidewalk. . . .

On Howard Street was a row of [wooden] frame . . . apartments. The outside wall of one building was in the street, exposing the rooms like a doll house. A few people were in the street in their night clothes and barefoot, crying, moaning, and wringing their hands.

Chase managed to get to the Ferry Building. Its south wall had fallen into the bay, and the clock tower on top of the building was unstable. In spite of the damage, Chase and a few coworkers opened up the office. By 7:00 A.M. they were doing a brisk business, selling hundreds of tickets to terrified San Franciscans hoping to flee by ferryboat to the city of Oakland, across the bay.

Unlike Cook, Hewitt, and Chase, most San Franciscans experienced the earthquake in their bedrooms, startled out of sleep into terror. James Hopper, a newspaper reporter for the *Call*, was sleeping restlessly in his apartment after an evening spent at the opera house. He had reviewed the opening performance of the Metropolitan Opera's production of *Carmen*, featuring world-renowned Italian tenor Enrico Caruso. His review would never be printed.

Hopper described how he "awoke to the city's destruction. Right away [the earthquake] was incredible. . . . It pounced upon the earth like a bulldog. . . . I heard the roar of bricks coming down, and twisted girders." Hopper ran to his third-floor window and gazed out on the chaos: "The St. Francis Hotel was waving to and fro with a swing as violent and exaggerated as a tree in a tempest. Then the rear of my building, for three stories upward, fell. The mass struck a series of little wooden houses in the alley below. I saw them crash in like emptied eggs, the bricks passing through the roofs as though through tissue paper. I had this feeling of finality. This is death."

All over the city San Franciscans were jolted awake by the initial shock of the massive earthquake. During the short pause before the more severe main shock, some remained in bed, terrified. Others dashed to doorways, believing that door frames would offer some protection against the bricks sure to rain down from collapsing chimneys. Many residents fell to their knees in prayer, hoping that they and their families would be spared as the jolting continued and the noise intensified. Some were certain that the end of the world was at hand.

Everywhere, residents heard the roaring of the earthquake, coupled with the ominous sounds of wood creaking, plaster falling, bricks crashing, steel groaning, and glass breaking. Some found themselves trapped in bedrooms behind shut doors that had become hopelessly stuck as houses lurched out of alignment. Many people were showered with falling plaster.

Emma Burke lived near Golden Gate Park in a wood-frame apartment. Her account probably reflects the experience of most San Franciscans living in well-constructed wooden buildings located on firm ground:

The shock came, and hurled my bed against an opposite wall. I sprang up, and holding firmly to the foot-board managed to keep on my feet to the door. The shock was constantly growing heavier; rumbles, crackling noises, and falling objects already commenced the din. . . . [My husband and I] braced ourselves in the doorway. . . .

We never knew when the chimney came tearing through; we never knew when a great marine picture weighing one hundred and twenty-five pounds crashed down, not eight feet away from us; we were frequently shaken loose from our hold on the door, and only kept our feet by mutual help and our utmost efforts; the floor moved like short, choppy waves of the sea, crisscrossed by a tide as mighty as themselves. The ceiling responded to all the angles of the floor. I never expected to come out alive.

City residents had even more harrowing experiences if they lived in brick buildings or in homes built on "made land" (ground created by adding soil and rubble to swampland or along a shoreline). Brick and cement structures throughout the city fell to pieces. Poorly built wood-frame houses constructed on unstable land collapsed or sank into liquefying, swampy ground. Hundreds lost their lives as buildings disintegrated, fell into one another, or tumbled into the street. One of the worst collapses involved the Brunswick Hotel, a large rooming house located south of Market Street. Hotel resident James Madison Jacobs recounted what happened to him when the earthquake struck:

> I jumped out of bed and made a grab for my clothes; but before I could get into them the second quake came. It was much more severe than the first and its effects were immediate and indescribable. There were noises of cracking, and rending, and shrieks and everything; and while these noises were terrorizing everybody, the building itself broke asunder into three parts. . . .One part pitched into Sixth Street, another into Howard Street, and the third section . . . remained standing.

Luckily, Jacobs had enough space in his mangled, debris-filled bedroom to pull on his clothes, despite the collapse of the floors and roof above him. He then tried to dig up and out of the devastation. He soon came across another resident pinned by some wooden beams. After Jacobs freed the man, the two climbed out of the wreckage, emerging onto part of the roof that had fallen over into Sixth Street. The survivors barely made their escape in time to avoid the flames already consuming the wrecked building. The blaze would kill scores of unlucky wounded trapped in the collapsed hotel.

Everywhere, terrified citizens burst from homes to

reach the perceived safety of the street. Some were dressed in nightclothes, and some were completely naked. Shortly after the shaking ceased, a guest at the Grand Hotel described the scene on Market Street:

> [It] was in a frightful state. Wires were down, naked and half naked men and women were running along the streets, cattle and horses were mixed up with the nude and the scene was one of indescribable confusion. Some we met were cut about the face and hands by falling glass or windows, and others had been hit by stones.

After the shaking stopped, residents began to survey the damage. Areas south of Market Street, including the Mission District, and places near San Francisco Bay were the hardest hit. Hundreds of wood-frame homes located there had been destroyed. Brick and cement buildings

The powerful temblor twisted these wood-frame structures at Ninth and Brannan Streets out of alignment or into mere piles of kindling.

Some of those startled out of sleep into terror found themselves pinned beneath the debris of their shattered homes. Hearing their frantic cries for help fill the dusty air, rescuers began the laborious task of locating and freeing the trapped victims.

throughout the city had been devastated, too. However, the newly constructed steel-frame skyscrapers on Market Street still stood, having escaped with little damage.

Eventually, stunned San Franciscans began mastering their fear. Some began cooking makeshift breakfasts for their families in the street. Others initiated rescue efforts, digging through precariously balanced debris to reach quake victims, whose terrified cries for help emanated from piles of rubble. Many stunned survivors stood silently, watching groups of local firefighters trying to put out the numerous blazes; overturned stoves, sparks from broken electric lines, and gas line explosions had caused more than 50 fires within the half hour following the quake.

James Hopper, the *Call* reporter, left his apartment to view damage to the city. As he headed to work at the Call

Building, he saw a wooden apartment building that had been devastated by debris raining down from the sky-scrapers on either side of it. Hopper noticed a man trying to escape from an upper window. The reporter dashed into the building and up the unsteady stairs with the intention of helping in the man's rescue: "I scrambled up to the third floor over piles of plaster and [wood], and there forgot about the man. For I came to a piece of room in which I found a bed covered with debris. A slim white hand and wrist reached out of the debris, like an appeal."

After a moment of shock, Hopper began uncovering the stricken woman, who was still alive. He gently carried her downstairs, and someone put her in a wagon bound for a hospital. Hopper then went back up into the building and found another injured woman, and then a dead woman under a pile of bricks. Soon he was joined by many other rescuers, and together they began digging out the body of a man who had been crushed to death in his bed beneath a mound of bricks.

The group worked for a while, picking up bricks one by one as if in a stupor. Then, as Hopper explained later, they realized the futility of their actions: "A red-headed youth who was digging with us said, 'What's de use of digging out those that's dead?' His remark struck us all as being so profoundly true that without another word, we all quit."

Earthquakes
and Science

The earthquake of 1906 split open the streets, toppling whatever lay in its path. Scientists would later measure openings as wide as 28 feet across in some places along the earthquake fault.

2

When the earthquake struck, most San Franciscans were not worrying about or even thinking of the cause of the terrible shaking they were experiencing. Most were too busy trying to stay on their feet, rush into the street, dodge falling masonry, or secure the safety of their family. But according to authors Gordon Thomas and Max Morgan Witts, just after the quake the residents of Chinatown encountered living proof—in the form of a frightened bull—that the very foundations of the earth had gone awry.

As Thomas and Witts describe in their book *The San Francisco Earthquake,* when Chinatown quake survivors saw a confused bull stumbling in the streets, they scattered in terror: "For many of the Chinese, the animal was the incarnation of their belief that the world was supported on the

Earthquake vibrations travel in waves. When strong enough, a temblor can move the earth, even bending trolley tracks into a wavelike pattern. Earthquake survivors who were inside buildings also saw this phenomenon. City resident Emma Burke recalled that "the floor moved like short, choppy waves of the sea, crisscrossed by a tide as mighty as themselves."

backs of four bulls. This was one of them—and in deserting his post he had caused the earth to tremble." Fearful residents hurled stones and knives at the bull, shouting at him to go back and rejoin his brothers supporting the world. Eventually a policeman shot the animal dead.

The Chinese belief that the frenzied bull was responsible for the earthquake was no stranger than some of the beliefs espoused by other city residents, clergymen, and scientists around the world after news of the San Francisco earthquake made international headlines. John Milne, a noted British expert on earthquakes, theorized, "Sometimes the earth gets a little bit off its course, and the reaction in swinging back to its true position involves a tremendous strain on the center. This is so great that it results in the breaking of the earth's crust." Another English scientist, Sir Hiram Maxim, claimed that the earth was gradually shrinking, and as it did so, the crust of the earth was cracking at its weakest points: "It will now be found that California is not so large as it was before the earthquake." An astrologer in France, Madame Simone Porodi, explained that "there is too much earth in the world." She predicted that soon whole sections of land would break off and fall into the sea.

Many priests and preachers, as well as laypeople, declared the earthquake to be an act of God. San Francisco had a deserved reputation in 1906 as a town where vice was prevalent. One district along the waterfront, known as the Barbary Coast, contained numerous saloons and houses of prostitution, and the city's Chinatown housed a number of brothels, opium dens, and gambling houses. Some religion-minded citizens felt that the city's destruction was a sign of God's judgment on the immoral town. However, after the earthquake a popular poem celebrating the survival of a liquor warehouse owned by A. P. Hotaling and Company reflected the amusement that most San Franciscans felt about that theory:

If, as some say, God spanked the town
For being over frisky,
Why did He burn the churches down
And save Hotaling's whisky?

Those skeptical San Franciscans would have been happy to know that earthquakes are natural phenomena. Their study, known as *seismology*, is based on knowledge of the earth's geological structure.

The earth is composed of multiple layers of material. At the center is the iron and nickel core, which is in turn surrounded by thick, dense, melted rock, called the mantle. On top of the mantle lies the *asthenosphere*. It is covered by the approximately 62-mile thick *lithosphere,* the solid outer layer of the earth. The lithosphere's outer surface is called the earth's *crust.*

In 1912 a German geologist named Alfred Wegener noticed something unusual about the earth's crust: South America and Africa looked like they should fit together like pieces in a puzzle. He concluded that the continents had once been joined but had gradually drifted apart. Unfortunately for Wegener, his theory of continental drift was largely ignored until the 1950s, when the discovery of ridges and trenches on the ocean floor led scientists to understand that the earth's crust is fractured, or divided into separate plates.

The 19 plates of the earth's crust are continuously moving, although at slow rates of only about two inches per year. When two plates move in opposite directions, and into each other, they can create a significant amount of friction. Sometimes the plates will simply slide past each other or get stuck; however, in other cases the plate edges will continue to push against each other, creating increasing tension and pressure until one side finally ruptures. This growing friction and violent release—called the *elastic-rebound* theory—causes an earthquake.

Plate boundaries are riddled with *faults,* which are weak areas and fractures in the earth's surface. The city of San Francisco lies close by one of the largest and most well-known faults in the world—the San Andreas Fault. In the 1906 quake, the San Andreas Fault ruptured for 280 miles. The rupture originated about 200 miles north of the city and raced south along the coastline at a speed of two miles per second. The land at the fault moved an average of 12 feet, and in some places as much as 28 feet.

During an earthquake, energy is released inside the earth at a point called the *focus* and then travels to the surface in *seismic waves.* In a severe earthquake this wavelike force can actually be visible. During the 1906 San Francisco quake some eyewitnesses reported seeing the earth itself moving in waves, and trolley tracks were bent into wavelike shapes.

Scientists measure and record earthquake vibrations using a special instrument called a *seismograph*. Seismologists —scientists who study earthquakes— record the vibrations of earthquakes as they occur, from anywhere in the world. By using seismograph data from three different locations, scientists can pinpoint the earthquake's *epicenter*—the place on the earth's surface directly above the focus of the earthquake.

Seismographs can also register the small foreshocks, or *precursors,* which are the vibrations that can occur just before a fault ruptures. Seismographs in Tokyo, Japan, registered precursors 23 minutes before the main shock hit San Francisco in 1906. It has been reported that animals seem to sense changes taking place inside the earth before a quake, which could explain why patrolman Jesse Cook noticed the restless horses at the marketplace minutes before the earthquake struck.

Hundreds of smaller aftershocks can occur after an earthquake hits, too, as the fault and the surrounding rock adjust to their new positions. Aftershocks began minutes after the major quake struck San Francisco, with a large aftershock hitting three hours later. In the following days and months residents would endure hundreds of aftershocks.

One of the world's most renowned seismologists, Dr. Charles Francis Richter (1900–85), watches as a seismograph records an earthquake's vibrations. Dr. Richter developed a scale that uses seismographic data to categorize an earthquake's size.

While nearby masonry buildings crumbled from the impact of the earthquake's powerful vibration, the unfinished steel skyscraper shown here remained upright and intact. Key to its survival was its construction of steel, a ductile, or flexible, material that could partially absorb the earth's movement.

Scientists also measure earthquakes by their force, or intensity, rating them by how much they affect people and by how much damage they cause. The closer a person is to the epicenter of the quake, the greater the damage and the greater the intensity that person experiences. At the time of the San Francisco earthquake, scientists used the Rossi-Forel scale of 1 to 10 to rate earthquake intensity, with 10 describing complete destruction. Professor Alexander McAdie, who in 1906 headed the U.S. Weather Bureau office in San Francisco and whose responsibility it was to keep a record of all earthquake shocks, rated the earthquake as a 9:

Earthquake No. 9 of the scale being used, is an earthquake which throws down badly built buildings and will give in the streets of the city a large amount of debris. It is about as severe an earthquake as can be experienced without total destruction, without great yawning chasms and complete destruction of life and property. The effect is more pronounced upon filled-in ground, loose soil, made land and alluvial soil, than upon rock formation.

Today the modified Mercalli scale is most commonly used to measure earthquake intensity. Developed by Giuseppe Mercalli in the early 20th century, the Mercalli scale ranks earthquakes by Roman numerals, from I to XII (see page 30). Based on information known about the 1906 quake, scientists today have rated its highest intensity at IX.

Years after the San Francisco earthquake, in 1935, seismologist Dr. Charles Richter proposed a scale that indicates an earthquake's magnitude, or the amount of energy it releases. In the Richter scale, each number represents a tenfold increase in the earthquake's vibrations and a thirtyfold increase in energy released: 1.5 indicates the smallest quake that can be felt; 4.5, a quake that causes slight damage; and 8.5, one that causes devastation. The largest earthquakes ever recorded are around 9 on the Richter scale.

Scientists have recently developed a new system, called the moment-magnitude scale, to measure very large earthquakes. Unlike the Richter scale, which compares data from seismograph readings worldwide, the moment-magnitude scale takes into account actual physical measurements of how much a fault moved. Although the Richter scale and moment-magnitude ratings are calculated differently, the numbers are comparable. For

MODIFIED MERCALLI INTENSITY SCALE

I. Not felt, except by a very few under especially favorable circumstances

II. Felt only by a few persons at rest, especially on upper floors of buildings

III. Felt quite noticeably indoors, especially on upper floors of buildings, but not recognized as an earthquake by many people; vibration like passing truck

IV. During the day felt indoors by many, outdoors by few; at night some awakened; dishes, windows, and doors disturbed; walls creak; sensation like heavy truck striking building

V. Felt by nearly everyone; many awakened; some dishes, windows, glassware break; some instances of cracked plaster; unstable objects overturn; some disturbance of trees, poles, and other tall objects

VI. Felt by all; many frightened and run outdoors; some heavy furniture moved; a few instances of fallen plaster or damaged chimneys; damage slight

VII. Everybody runs outdoors; damage negligible in buildings of good design and construction, slight to moderate in well-built ordinary structures, considerable in poorly built or badly designed structures; some chimneys break

VIII. Damage slight in specially designed structures, considerable in ordinary substantial buildings, great in poorly built structures; chimneys, factory stacks, columns, monuments, and walls fall; heavy furniture overturns

IX. Damage considerable in specially designed structures and great in substantial buildings, with partial collapse; well-designed frame structures thrown out of alignment; buildings shift off foundations and ground cracks conspicuously; underground pipes break

X. Some well-built wooden structures destroyed; most masonry and frame structures destroyed with foundations; ground cracks badly; rails bend; riverbanks and steep slopes have landslides; sand and mud shift

XI. Few, if any, masonry structures remain standing; bridges destroyed; broad, deep cracks open in ground; underground pipelines completely out of service; earth slumps and land slips in soft ground; rails bend greatly

XII. Damage total; practically all works of construction are severely damaged or destroyed; seismic waves visible on ground surfaces; lines of sight and level distorted; objects thrown upward into the air

Adapted from:
Halacy, D. S., Jr. Earthquakes. Indianapolis: Bobbs-Merrill, 1974 and Levy, Matthys and Mario Salvadori. Why the Earth Quakes. New York: W. W. Norton, 1995.

example, the 1906 San Francisco earthquake is rated as 7.7 on the Richter scale and 7.9 on the moment-magnitude scale. Earthquake experts generally compromise and give the quake a 7.8 rating.

An earthquake's magnitude does not always reflect how much destruction it causes. The extent of quake damage depends on several factors, such as how close the epicenter is to densely populated areas, the design and construction of affected buildings, the type of soil they are built on, and the length of the tremor.

The epicenter of the 1906 earthquake was near San Francisco. That explains why the damage was so much worse in that city than in Oakland, which was just a few miles away across San Francisco Bay.

A building's shape can determine whether it survives an earthquake. Symmetrical structures will vibrate without twisting, whereas asymmetrical structures will twist. To withstand a severe temblor, buildings must be made of material that is ductile, or flexible. Steel is such a material, and the new steel-frame skyscrapers that had just been built in turn-of-the-century San Francisco proved their worth by surviving the quake with minimal damage. The worst building material in earthquake-prone areas is masonry—brick, cinder blocks, or concrete. It is so stiff that earthquakes just shake it down. Reinforced concrete—concrete with an internal steel frame—is a significantly better material than unreinforced concrete.

The earthquake damage sustained by buildings throughout San Francisco illustrated these points. Chimneys, steeples, and towers—such as those found on City Hall and the Ferry Building—are asymmetrical features. Because they twist as they vibrate, unlike the rest of the building, they are generally the first structures to succumb to earthquake shaking. An estimated 95 percent of the chimneys in San Francisco fell or sustained damage in the

The devastation of the Valencia Hotel, in which most residents of the boardinghouse perished, resulted from several factors: the unstable land upon which the structure was built, its wooden structure, and its location near the epicenter of the quake. The four-story building actually sank three stories in liquefied ground before collapsing.

earthquake. Most were constructed of brick. While steel-frame and reinforced-masonry structures survived the earthquake intact, unreinforced masonry structures lost entire walls, which were effectively sheared off. Since wood is a fairly ductile material, well-built wood-frame buildings on solid ground survived the quake fairly well, with some damage to the plaster walls.

When constructed on unstable ground, however, wood-frame buildings (especially those of poor construction) were not so lucky. Soft sand and mud slow earthquake waves down and concentrate them, increasing the intensity of the earthquake, and thus the damage.

Although San Francisco is famous for its steep streets

and hilly terrain, the city was also developed on "made land." Trash and rubble had been dumped along the bay shoreline and into Mission Bay Swamp, then covered with a thin layer of sand and earth. This filled ground in the Mission District and south of Market Street was developed with poorly constructed buildings, warehouses, factories, rooming houses—and even City Hall.

If vibrations in a swampy or sandy area go on long enough, the ground can actually liquefy, causing buildings to sink. The effects of liquefaction were graphically seen in the collapse of the four-story Valencia Hotel in the Mission District. During the earthquake the hotel sank three stories and then collapsed. The fourth floor was left at ground level. Survivors of the hotel's collapse believed that as many as 200 people were killed there.

Another factor that affects earthquake damage is the length of the tremor. The 1906 earthquake lasted 45 to 60 seconds, a very long earthquake. However great the damage caused by the tremor and its aftershocks was, though, the earthquake itself was only the beginning of a major disaster for San Francisco. Next would come an even deadlier catastrophe—one of the worst ever to strike an American city.

Flames sweep through Market Street in uncontrollable fury. Within minutes after the quake, the sparks and explosions from downed electrical wires and broken gas lines ignited small fires. Because the temblor also damaged water mains and disabled hydrants, firefighters could not prevent the flames from spreading.

Fire! 3

Wednesday, April 18

Rescuers soon became discouraged as they found the task of digging out the dead and injured just too monumental and too dangerous. Aftershocks continued to shake down loose wreckage, and the small fires that had started immediately after the quake were spreading, threatening to scorch victims and rescuers alike.

Then grim reality hit both residents and firefighters, and their initial relief at having escaped death by earthquake was replaced by a new fear. Everywhere they turned, survivors could see flames roaring out of nearby buildings or ominous plumes of black smoke rising in the distance. Water from broken mains rushed in torrents down the street. Some residents smelled gas, and explosions from broken gas mains ruptured the pavement, injuring and even killing passersby.

Firemen tried hooking up their hoses to hydrant after hydrant, but to no avail. Almost all of the water mains were broken. At best, hydrants yielded a trickle, but usually there was no water at all. The fires were spreading, and firemen had no water.

Firefighters had no system of communication, either. No alarms sounded in the silent city, as the central fire alarm system had been destroyed. Telephone and telegraph lines did not function. Firemen had no way of knowing, besides using their eyes, where the fires were, and no means of coordinating fire control efforts.

Brigadier General Frederick Funston, the acting commanding officer of the Army's Pacific Division in San Francisco, was asleep at his home on Nob Hill when the earthquake struck. Shaken awake by the tremor, he dressed immediately and rushed outside to survey the damage. From his vantage point above the city, Funston could see smoke rising from numerous areas. Then, as he walked down California Street toward the waterfront, he discovered that the firefighters had no water. Funston quickly realized that much, if not all, of the city could be lost to a huge conflagration. Believing that the scope of the disaster would be well beyond the ability of the police and fire departments to handle, he decided to order in troops.

Because the telephone lines were inoperable, Funston ran to the army stables, about a mile away on Pine Street. Along the way he asked a city patrolman to inform police chief Jeremiah Dinan that troops would soon be arriving. Upon reaching the stables, Funston sent his carriage driver with messages to the commanding officers of the closest army garrisons—Fort Mason (on the north end of Van Ness Avenue) and the Presidio (on the city outskirts). He asked the officers to report with all available troops to the police chief at the Hall of Justice, the city's administrative offices, located in Portsmouth Square.

The commanding officer at Fort Mason, Captain Walker, quickly mustered his troops, who were on their way to the Hall of Justice by 7:00 A.M. Some accounts report that the commanding officer of the Presidio, Col. Charles Morris, was much less cooperative. As the story goes, Morris greeted Funston's orders with incredulity and rage: "Go back and tell [Funston] that he had better look up his army regulations, and there he will find that nobody but the President of the United States in person can order regular troops into any city!"

Whether or not that story is true, Morris and his troops arrived in San Francisco shortly after the troops from Fort Mason. However, Morris's alleged statement does contain a significant grain of truth: it *was* illegal and unconstitutional for Funston to order troops into San Francisco. Many would later hail Funston as a hero for his quick and decisive action in dealing with the disaster, but others would criticize him for the liberties he took with the law in his unilateral decision to order in troops.

General Funston would not be the only decision-maker to endure criticism for his illegal actions during the crisis. San Francisco's mayor, Eugene Schmitz, also saw the need for immediate action. Soon after the quake struck, Mayor Schmitz met with police chief Jeremiah

Brigadier General Frederick Funston was serving as acting commander of the U.S. Army's Pacific Division on April 18, 1906, the day of the quake. The general immediately called in troops, an action considered illegal by some, although most people credit him with helping save San Francisco from total chaos.

A copy of the official proclamation by Mayor Eugene Schmitz, posted by nightfall the day of the earthquake. Many believed that the order to shoot looters was illegal and carried out without justice.

PROCLAMATION
BY THE MAYOR

The Federal Troops, the members of the Regular Police Force and all Special Police Officers have been authorized by me to KILL any and all persons found engaged in Looting or in the Commission of Any Other Crime.

I have directed all the Gas and Electric Lighting Co.'s not to turn on Gas or Electricity until I order them to do so. You may therefore expect the city to remain in darkness for an indefinite time.

I request all citizens to remain at home from darkness until daylight every night until order is restored.

I WARN all Citizens of the danger of fire from Damaged or Destroyed Chimneys, Broken or Leaking Gas Pipes or Fixtures, or any like cause.

E. E. SCHMITZ, Mayor

Dated, April 18, 1906.

ALTVATER PRINT, MISSION AND 3RD STS.

Dinan and acting fire chief John Dougherty. They set up makeshift disaster headquarters in the basement of the Hall of Justice, despite the fact that the building's badly damaged tower was in danger of collapse. Schmitz quickly dispatched telegrams to California's governor, George C. Pardee, and to Mayor Mott of Oakland, requesting assistance.

When the troops from Fort Mason and the Presidio

arrived at the Hall of Justice, Mayor Schmitz startled them with the directness of his orders: in addition to keeping citizens back from the fire and guarding the $6 million in the treasury at City Hall, the soldiers were to shoot to kill anyone caught looting or committing any other serious crime. Of his decision to issue these highly illegal orders, Schmitz later wrote, "Anticipating that looting would take place . . . and realizing that we would have no place in which to keep prisoners if we arrested any, and that it was time for firm and decisive action, I told [the commanding officers] to let the news be widely spread that anyone caught looting should not be arrested but should be shot."

Schmitz also gave an equally illegal, but much less controversial, order to police chief Dinan. He requested that the 700-man police force close down all establishments that sold liquor. The mayor was concerned that drunkenness would only worsen the chaos that was already gripping the city. The military troops would also assist the police in the effort to ban the sale of alcohol.

Few would argue against the need for Schmitz's anti-alcohol order, but the order to shoot looters would be a source of endless controversy after the disaster. By evening, copies of the official proclamation informing citizens of the shoot-to-kill order, and about the dangers of fire from damaged chimneys, pipes, and fixtures, would be posted throughout the city.

Soon realizing that the normal channels of city government were not equipped to handle a large-scale disaster, Mayor Schmitz invited approximately 50 prominent citizens to meet at the Hall of Justice at 3 P.M. to form a Committee of Safety, soon to be known as the Committee of Fifty. Surprisingly, he did not invite his crony, lawyer Abe Ruef, who was the city's political boss. Schmitz did, however, include several of his enemies—men who

Firefighters dash to the next blaze. In 1906, the chief method of firefighting was horse-drawn fire engines, used to pump water from the hydrants and from underground reservoirs, or cisterns, located throughout San Francisco. Unfortunately, firemen found working hydrants in only a few, rare instances, and available cisterns were soon drained dry.

wished to indict him and Ruef on criminal charges.

During his tenure as mayor, Schmitz had shown no signs of integrity. He was the tool of Abe Ruef, who directed, encouraged, and benefited from the corruption prevalent in the Schmitz administration. In fact, the day before the earthquake, Schmitz had learned that he and Ruef were to be investigated on charges of bribery (taking money in exchange for favors or influence) and graft (illegal gain of power or money).

In the days following the earthquake, however, Schmitz would not display any concern about the impending investigation or show any desire to use the disaster to line his pockets. He would make key decisions without soliciting input from Abe Ruef. Schmitz would seem the perfect leader, taking decisive action and dedicating his every waking hour to the welfare of his city. And now the threat of fire was a major concern.

Unfortunately, the mayor's acting fire chief, John Dougherty, was still recovering from two shocks: the earthquake itself and his unexpected promotion. Fire chief Dennis Sullivan had been mortally injured during the earthquake when a chimney from a neighboring hotel crashed into his quarters in the fire station. The loss of their leader was an additional blow to the 585 members of the fire department, already badly disorganized by the destruction of communications and demoralized by the lack of water.

Dougherty tried to devise a plan to curtail the fires, but this would prove to be almost impossible to execute. The department had no means of communication available except horse or foot power. And the horse-drawn fire engines and hose wagons from companies throughout the city had already headed off toward the nearest blaze.

Conditions were particularly bad in the residential, working-class area south of Market Street, where dozens of fires had sprung up. The individual blazes quickly combined into an immense conflagration moving in all directions.

Firefighters fought this "South of Market" fire on all fronts. To the north, Acting Chief Dougherty hoped to use the width of Market Street as a firebreak—a cleared space where nothing can burn, thus stopping the fire's advance. To the east, fireboats in the bay pumped salt water onto the Ferry Building and attempted to prevent fires from spreading to crucial oceanfront warehouses. To the south and west, firefighters battled the fire every block of its advance.

The growing inferno in the South of Market area was not the city's only worry. Multiple fires had also broken out north of Market Street, in the produce and wholesale district. This commercial downtown area also contained most of the city's theaters and hotels, as well as financial and retail businesses.

As if these two main areas of conflagration—one south and one north of Market Street—were not enough, the situation worsened by midmorning when another fire broke out in the Hayes Valley section of the city, about five blocks from City Hall. Legend has it that the fire began when a woman tried to cook breakfast for her hungry family. Unaware that her chimney was damaged, she lit her stove. A spark from the damaged flue set her chimney and roof afire, setting off a new blaze, aptly dubbed the Ham and Eggs Fire.

Firefighters stopped the blaze at its northern and western boundaries with the aid of a working hydrant. But then the Ham and Eggs Fire turned south, heading for the Mission District, the oldest part of San Francisco, and east, threatening the business district around Market Street.

✦   ✦   ✦

At the same time, the South of Market conflagration was quickly moving west, also threatening the Mission District. With no water, firefighters could do little more than retreat, leaving behind hundreds of doomed people trapped in the rubble of fallen rooming houses.

Desperate to delay the progress of the growing inferno, firefighters were ready to try anything that had a chance of creating a firebreak. So, although untrained in the use of dynamite, the men obtained explosives from the nearby Southern Pacific rail yards, on Townsend Street, and attempted to dynamite a firebreak at Eighth Street. Unfortunately, the amateurish dynamiting did

nothing to check the fire. It may even have hastened the relentless fire's advance by hurling burning wreckage ahead of the flames.

By noon the northern edge of the South of Market fire had reached Market Street, home to some of the premiere businesses in San Francisco and the greatest collection of modern steel-frame skyscrapers in the entire West. Frustrated firefighters kept on battling the flames, hoping to prevent the fire from jumping Market Street and continuing north. But the desperate men needed water, and only a few sources were available: bay water being pumped by fireboats (used mostly to protect the Ferry Building at the foot of Market Street) and one hydrant connected to a private saltwater supply for downtown

By Wednesday afternoon, the South of Market fire had engulfed the business section of Market Street. There the elegant Palace Hotel, which had already proven itself earthquake-proof, stood ready with its own water supply to withstand the flames. However, by late afternoon, even the "fireproof" Palace Hotel had been lost.

bathhouses. But then firefighters learned of yet another source—the private freshwater stock of the Palace Hotel.

The pride of San Francisco, the elegant, 800-room Palace Hotel was one of the largest in the world. Built to be both earthquake-proof and fireproof, the hotel contained its own emergency supply of water, which the Palace employees planned to use to save the luxury hotel.

However, the creators of the hotel's fire defenses had not counted on the desperation of the firefighters, who tapped into and soon drained the Palace's water supply. Although bay water eventually saved the Ferry Building at the foot of Market Street, nothing could save the buildings on the south side of the street. By midafternoon all were in flames, including the Palace Hotel, the last to burn.

Updates on the dire situation in the city that day were communicated to the outside world through the one functioning telegraph line in San Francisco. Despite the earthquake and the encroaching flames, a courageous telegrapher at the Postal Telegraph Office at the corner of Market and Montgomery Streets kept the world informed of the worsening situation until early afternoon. Finally the advancing flames forced him to abandon his post. Near 2:30 P.M. the telegrapher sent his final message:

> The city practically ruined by fire. It's within half block of us in the same block. The Call building is burned out entirely, the Examiner building just fell in a heap. Fire all around in every direction and way out in residence district. Destruction by earthquake something frightful. The City Hall Dome stripped and only the framework standing. The St. Ignatius Church and College are burned to the ground. The Emporium is gone, entire building, also the Old Flood Building. Lots of new buildings just recently finished

are completely destroyed. They are blowing standing buildings that are in the path of flames up with dynamite. No water. It's awful. There is no communication anywhere and entire phone system is busted. I want to get out of here or be blown up.

Chief Operator Postal Telegraph Office

San Francisco, Cal. 2:20 P.M.

The situation on Market Street was worsened by the threat of the Ham and Eggs Fire, which by late afternoon was approaching Market Street from the west. It now threatened the sick and injured patients of the Central Emergency Hospital, who had been evacuated to nearby Mechanics Hall, an old wooden arena still colorfully decorated for the Mardi Gras roller-skating festival held there just 12 hours earlier. In a short time the makeshift hospital had been flooded with injured quake victims. Now the Ham and Eggs Fire bore down on the hall and its occupants.

Although the hospital doctors and nurses had little time to evacuate, they managed to save their patients, with significant help from passersby and the use of donated and commandeered horses, wagons, and automobiles. The injured were taken to other hospitals and to a newly established refugee camp at Golden Gate Park, where an open-air hospital had been set up. Later, rumors would persist that as many as several hundred wounded were left behind in the panic to escape, but eyewitnesses to the evacuation would angrily refute such charges.

The Ham and Eggs Fire soon devastated Mechanics Hall. The blaze then engulfed City Hall, sending greedy tongues of flame throughout the earthquake-ravaged building and destroying all of the precious records stored there. The loss of documentation of births, marriages, deaths, and property rights would complicate life for the city's residents for decades to come.

Meanwhile, the southern edge of the South of Market fire held until mid-afternoon—assisted by the lucky find of a working hydrant at Sixth and Folsom. When that water gave out, firefighters pumped from the sewers, which were full of water from broken mains. But the inferno eventually grew too large to be contained by their small streams of water, and the flames resumed their inexorable march southward.

In their path lay the Southern Pacific rail yards, which firefighters were determined to protect at Townsend Street. If the rail yards burned, no refugees could leave San Francisco by rail. Fire had already trapped hundreds in the rail yards. They couldn't flee the city because the railroad was not yet running, and any avenue of escape had been cut off by the blaze.

✝   ✝   ✝

North of Market, the fire in the produce and wholesale district was moving more slowly. But it continued to steadily devour blocks to the west and the south. And at 3 P.M. it was closing in on the Hall of Justice, where the Committee of Fifty members had gathered. The men hurriedly agreed to meet next time at the Fairmont Hotel, several blocks away from the fire. As the hall shook with the blasts of nearby dynamiting, the nervous members fled the building and continued the session outdoors, in nearby Portsmouth Square. The committee would change meeting locations several times in the following days as the fires advanced, consuming block after block of the city.

Dynamite saw widespread use in the battle against the "North of Market" fire. Without water there was no alternative but to demolish buildings to create firebreaks. Unfortunately, Mayor Schmitz, fearful of outcries from

property owners, gave permission for soldiers to dynamite only the buildings "in immediate contact with those already ablaze." No effective firebreak could be established so close to the flames, and as it had in the South of Market area, the blasting often succeeded only in setting additional buildings on fire.

Even worse than dynamite was black powder. Whereas dynamite detonates with little flame, black powder produces large flames when it explodes. Although the army officers in charge of demolition, Lieutenant Briggs and Captain Coleman, were aware of this fact, they were under pressure to act. So when the dynamite ran out, they reluctantly began using black powder.

That evening firefighters tried to stop the westward direction of the North of Market fire by making a stand at Kearny Street. Unfortunately, when soldiers set

The Ham and Eggs Fire spread quickly through the Hayes Valley area and then devastated City Hall, whose dome appears in the center background of this photograph. The fire destroyed all paperwork documenting the 60-year history of the city, including birth and death certificates, as well as property wills and deeds.

Some evacuees of the Central Emergency Hospital retreated from the Ham and Eggs Fire to a refugee camp established at Golden Gate Park. At a makeshift hospital in the park, a doctor administers treatment to an injured patient.

off a black-powder charge in one building, flaming bedding flew out the upstairs window onto the other side of Kearny. Not only had they failed to stop the fire, but its flames now threatened the wooden buildings of Chinatown, the city's most densely populated district. Its thousands of residents would have to evacuate—quickly.

✚   ✚   ✚

Around the same time, the ongoing fight against the South of Market fire along Townsend Street received a welcome boost from navy sailors, who piloted a boat up a city water channel to bring much-needed freshwater to the firefighters and refugees trapped at the Southern Pacific rail yards. From the fireboat *Leslie,* sailors pumped salt water through a hose that stretched from the bay to Eighth and Townsend Streets. According to the official navy report filed by the commanding officer, Lieutenant Frederick Freeman, the fire at Townsend Street was under control by 2:30 the following morning. The Southern Pacific rail yards were safe.

Other hopeful developments were reported to Mayor Schmitz from the wasteland of the South of Market area. Government employees had managed to save two key buildings—the U.S. Post Office (at Seventh and Mission) and the U.S. Mint (at Fifth and Mission). Although soldiers had ordered the post office employees from the building, 10 workers remained behind and beat out the flames with wet mail sacks.

The fight to save the U.S. Mint took considerably more manpower. Approximately 50 employees stayed to battle the fire, under the direction of Superintendent Frank A. Leach, who had come over on the bay ferry that morning from his home in Oakland. The Mint employees received some help from soldiers who had been assigned to guard both the building and the $300 million in gold and silver stored in its vaults. The building's fire-resistant iron shutters and granite construction, along with the water supplied by an artesian well, helped the determined workers declare victory over the fire at 5 P.M.

Unfortunately, good news like this was scarce. On Wednesday evening, hopes of saving several blocks in the wholesale district, on the north side of Market Street, were dashed when yet another fire sprang up. Most reports say it began in the ruins of the Delmonico Restaurant, on O'Farrell Street, where some soldiers had stopped to cook dinner. Their cooking fire spread quickly in the ruined building, erupting into a blaze that would be referred to as the Delmonico Fire. By midnight, it had combined with the northeastern arm of the Ham and Eggs Fire and the North of Market fire to produce an even larger conflagration, moving due west.

A Colossal Conflagration

Firemen aim an arc of water at a block of burning buildings in an attempt to slow the fire's advance. When no water was available, firefighters used more drastic techniques, such as dynamiting—destroying whole blocks of buildings at a time in order to create firebreaks.

4

Thursday, April 19

As the relentless flames spread, terrified residents were fleeing the area with as much as they could carry. Families with wagons and sacks of precious belongings hurried grimly toward the open areas of safety in the city's parks, or down Market Street toward the Ferry Building, hoping to flee the devastated city by boat.

On Wednesday, the block-long park at Union Square had quickly become a camp for hundreds of weary refugees. Although close to Market Street, the open area was thought to be well out of danger from the North of Market fires. In spite of the lack of water, city residents could not imagine that their heroic fire department would not find a way to halt

Author Jack London, whose adventure novels had made him the most widely read author in America at the time, wrote an article about the earthquake's aftermath for *Collier's* magazine. London's "The Story of an Eyewitness" was published two weeks after the disaster.

the advance of the menacing flames.

A famous eyewitness would later relate the drama of Union Square to the world. Jack London, author of *Call of the Wild* and *White Fang,* felt the tremor Wednesday morning at his ranch 40 miles from San Francisco. Curious about the earthquake's effect on the city, he and his wife came to survey the damage. In his article about the disaster, published in the May 5 issue of *Collier's* magazine,

London described the Union Square camp: "At eight o'clock Wednesday evening I passed through Union Square. It was packed with refugees. Thousands of them had gone to bed on the grass. Government tents had been set up, supper was being cooked, and the refugees were lining up for free meals."

But late Wednesday night, after the Delmonico Fire erupted and combined with other fires, the resulting towering mass of flames meant Union Square was no longer a safe haven. London describes how the scene at the park drastically changed within just a few hours: "At half past one in the morning three sides of Union Square were in flames. The fourth side, where stood the great St. Francis Hotel, was still holding out. An hour later, ignited from top and sides, the St. Francis was flaming heavenward. Union Square, heaped high with mountains of trunks, was deserted. Troops, refugees, and all had retreated."

The citizens and troops in the park at Union Square had been taken completely by surprise by the quick westward advance of the fire. Many refugees in the square had arrived in total exhaustion, having spent hours dragging heavy trunks and other belongings through the streets. Suddenly, in the early morning hours, the soldiers woke up the fatigued men, women, and children and forced them to evacuate. In a hurried retreat from the threatening inferno, most were forced to abandon the precious possessions they had painstakingly lugged about the previous day.

✚   ✚   ✚

Firefighters hoped to stop the advancing flames at Powell Street. They believed that the now vacated Union Square offered a bit of a firebreak, as did several empty lots along the length of the street.

However, the fire soon jumped Powell and began scorching a relentless path up the eastern slope of Nob Hill. Located here were the expensive and lavishly decorated homes of San Francisco's most prominent and wealthiest families—those who had made their fortunes from gold and silver mining and from the railroad industry. For several hours firefighters attempted to save the ostentatious mansions of Nob Hill's millionaires, but the little water the firefighters could find in the city's underground cisterns soon ran dry. Millions of dollars in priceless art, china, rug, and furniture collections held in these palaces of the rich soon went up in smoke.

Before the fire destroyed the homes on Nob Hill, Jack London spent some time there, watching the flames approach. He described the wistful resignation displayed by the neighborhood's wealthy residents:

> On Thursday morning at a quarter past five, just twenty-four hours after the earthquake, I sat on the steps of a small residence on Nob Hill. . . . All about were the palaces of the nabob [rich] . . . . To the east and south at right angles, were advancing two mighty walls of flame.
>
> I went inside with the owner of the house on the steps of which I sat. He was cool and cheerful and hospitable. "Yesterday morning," he said, "I was worth six hundred thousand dollars. This morning this house is all I have left. It will go in fifteen minutes." He pointed to a large cabinet. "That is my wife's collection of china. This rug upon which we stand is a present. It cost fifteen hundred dollars. Try that piano. Listen to its tone. There are few like it. There are no horses [to haul these goods away]. The flames will be here in fifteen minutes."

As Thursday morning dawned, the flames were advancing on two main fronts. South of Market, the fire was edging farther south into the Mission District. North of Market, the flames were moving up and over Nob Hill, westward toward the expensive homes on Van Ness Avenue, and northward toward the wooden buildings on Russian Hill, the highest point in the city. To the east this fire was also setting the narrow alleys and combustible tenement houses of Chinatown ablaze.

The confidence and hope that had been in evidence on Wednesday a few hours after the earthquake were now completely gone. Most citizens were convinced that the entire city would burn. The military had closed the stricken city to outsiders. Few people were entering; instead, all over San Francisco, refugees hurried to escape. By noon on Thursday, crowds of refugees were pouring down the burned, smoking wasteland of Market Street to the Ferry Building, where they waited in long lines for the Oakland ferry. Some evacuees escaped by rail on the Southern Pacific railway, which carried them at no charge; others paid exorbitant fees to hire a boat to take them to Oakland.

Many people, afraid to go anywhere near the fire, walked miles west to the main refugee camps in Golden Gate Park and at the Presidio. Determined to save as much as possible, the displaced residents dragged trunks for miles and improvised conveyances for their possessions. As they walked and their trunks, sacks, and bags grew heavier and heavier, they would cast off possessions to lighten their load. Eyewitnesses commented on the sheer variety of prized possessions that determined refugees dragged from their doomed homes. Pianos and caged birds were two fairly common, although impractical, sights. In the August 1906 issue of *The New Century Magazine,* Louise Herrick Wall described the scene:

> The sidewalks, already almost impassable with wreckage, were filled for miles . . . with household goods of

Trunks, sacks, and bags surround exhausted refugees, who sit guarding the household goods and treasured possessions they rescued before fleeing from the fires.

every known variety: sewing machines, wads of bedding, pans, dishes, mirrors . . . bureaus, beds, pianos, banjos, soup tureens. . . . Everything that moved on wheel or castor became a wagon. Baby carriages, piled high with clothes and bedding, sometimes running upon a single wheel, and trunks with castors, or two or three trunks a-tandem, were drawn through the streets by ropes of torn sheets. Women with lapdogs and hundreds of men and women with bird cages— parrots, canaries, and love-birds—hurried with the hurrying caravan.

Once the refugees reached the safety of the city's various parks, most received aid. By Thursday organized relief efforts were beginning. Food, water, and bedding were being distributed by volunteers and the army at Golden Gate Park and the Presidio, as well as at several smaller parks scattered throughout unburned areas.

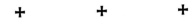

Very early Thursday morning, firefighters, the military, and Mayor Schmitz had realized that their last line of defense against the North of Market fire was Van Ness Avenue, a 125-foot-wide boulevard running north-south, nearly seven blocks west of Nob Hill. Fearing that fighting the flames on the narrow streets between Nob Hill and Van Ness would be hopeless, authorities had instead evacuated all the residents. Blocks of the city were abandoned to the flames as the fire finished off the remainder of the downtown area.

By early Thursday afternoon, the North of Market fire was closing in on the well-to-do homes along Van Ness Avenue. To halt the raging inferno, Captain Coleman, who was in charge of dynamiting, and General Funston believed it would be necessary to dynamite homes on the east side of Van Ness. This would widen the firebreak provided by the broad avenue. Mayor Schmitz reluctantly agreed to the desperate measure. He knew that the Van Ness mansions housed some very wealthy residents (although not as wealthy as those burned out on Nob Hill), and he hated to make a decision that would place himself in conflict with them. However, Schmitz—and most people—realized that the fire was so huge that drastic measures had to be taken or the entire city would be lost to the flames.

Soldiers began backfiring and dynamiting along some areas of Van Ness Avenue. Backfiring involves setting small fires that will burn available fuel before the main fire gets there, causing the main fire to peter out for lack of fuel. The success of this tactic depends on keeping the backfires from growing out of control.

James Stetson, who witnessed much of the fight on Van Ness Avenue from his home, described the soldiers' rather haphazard methods of backfiring: "A soldier would, with a vessel like a fruit-dish in his hand, containing some inflammable stuff, enter the house, climb to the second floor, go to the front window, open it, pull down the shade and curtain, and set fire to the contents of his dish. In a short time the shades and curtain would be in a blaze. When the fire started slowly, to give it a draught [the men] would throw bricks and stones up to the windows to break the glass."

Although the backfires soon raged out of control, firefighters managed to keep the flames from making any inroads into the west side of Van Ness Avenue for quite some time. To the south, water was available from a working hydrant at Buchanan Street and Golden Gate Avenue. To the north, fire engines pumped water from a hose that ran several blocks down Van Ness Avenue from the bay. By Thursday evening the fire had been successfully halted south of Sutter Street. But then, horrified firefighters watched as the flames defiantly leaped the broad avenue, crossing onto the west side of Van Ness. The last line of defense had been broken.

Although discouraged, the men struggled on. They knew that the survival of this newly threatened residential area, known as the Western Addition, depended on their success. They quickly dynamited a new firebreak on the next parallel road, Franklin Street. Firemen climbed to the roofs of nearby buildings to rip off burning shingles with their bare hands. Their efforts were aided by the water from a working fire hydrant at Buchanan Street and a change in the wind, which began to blow from the west, pushing the fire back over itself.

Finally, many hours later, on early Friday morning, firefighters managed to stop the wall of flame after it had burned only six blocks west of Van Ness. Through their desperate and heroic efforts, the men had saved the remainder of the Western Addition.

Unfortunately, the fire was still moving to the north. The weary firefighters' task was not yet over.

✛   ✛   ✛

On Thursday night, fires continued to ravage Chinatown as winds drove the blaze eastward. Flames now threatened the Appraiser's Building and the Montgomery Block, an area that on the previous day had been threatened by fires from the south. Under the leadership of Lieutenant Frederick Freeman, marines and sailors worked together with firemen and citizens to halt the fire's relentless advance. Their defense was a small stream of bay water shooting from an 11-block-long hose that ran back to the U.S. Navy tug *Leslie*. The fireboat pumped steadily throughout the night, until finally the Montgomery Block was saved for a second time.

The fire department's small fire engines were no match for the huge conflagrations engulfing the city of San Francisco, yet the firefighters were determined to prevail. They continuously searched for water—from working hydrants, cisterns, private supplies, and the San Francisco Bay.

"A Roaring Fury of Flame"

Friday, April 20

On Friday morning Mayor Schmitz was beginning to feel some optimism. The fire that had crossed Van Ness Avenue had been stopped at Franklin Street. Assuming the Western Addition was now out of danger, Schmitz sent a telegraph to the War Department informing U.S. government officials that the San Francisco fire was under control. He made the same announcement that afternoon to the public: "To the Citizens of San Francisco," his proclamation began. "The fire is now under control and all danger is past."

Schmitz was quite wrong. The Mission District was still burning. Flames were sweeping the Italian neighborhoods on Telegraph Hill, remnants of the fire that had claimed Chinatown the day before. And although the westward progress of the blaze had been halted at Van Ness Avenue, the fire was still burning fiercely northward. Earlier that morning, firefighters had tried to hold those flames at Green Street and Van Ness by using dynamite.

Once again, however, poor use of explosives had a major negative effect. Embers from a dynamited building on the south side of Green Street set the north side of the road aflame. As Mayor Schmitz was writing his optimistic telegram to the War Department and readying his proclamation to the public, the fire was racing up unburned sections of Russian Hill and into the North Beach area. Until now North Beach had been considered out of danger, and its residents had not been evacuated.

As had been the case since the fires began, little could be done without water. What water there was in North Beach came from cisterns, which were soon drained dry, or from the bay, pumped by fireboats to protect the wharves. Some water was pumped a few blocks inland by hose in hopes of saving the warehouses near Telegraph Hill.

To evacuate the North Beach refugees, 16 men and two officers from the USS *Chicago* orchestrated a tremendous rescue effort. Impressing into service every floating craft it could find, the navy evacuated as many as 20,000 people from the threatening inferno, ferrying them to safety across the bay to the city of Sausalito. Newspaper reports would later claim that more than a hundred people from North Beach burned to death in their homes and in the streets because they could not escape the flames that swiftly engulfed the area. The truth of that has never been, and never will be, determined.

On Russian Hill, half of which had burned on Thursday, some resourceful residents were prepared for the fire's onslaught. Defying evacuation orders, they had remained behind to save their homes. Some of them succeeded, using buckets of water or wine, wet sacks and cloths, and even their bare hands to put out the flames. One home on Russian Hill that escaped destruction had a survival story that circulated widely after the fire. Called the House of the Flag, it became a symbol of the defiant spirit of San Francisco's citizens.

As the story goes, the Sheppard family had laid in a supply of water, determined to prevent the flames from destroying their home. However, when ordered by the army to evacuate, the Sheppards reluctantly left. Remaining behind was Edward A. Dakin, a Civil War veteran and historical flag collector who rented part of the home. But even he lost hope as the fire drew closer, the heat grew more intense, and finally the wood of the house began to smoke. As a final gesture before abandoning the house, Dakin ran one of his American flags up the roof flagpole and dipped it three times in farewell to the house and to the San Francisco he had known. Then he left.

Unbeknownst to Mr. Dakin, a company of soldiers patrolling Russian Hill saw the flag and the signal. They decided, perhaps in a patriotic fervor, to save the house. Using the water the Sheppards had stockpiled and wet sand from a nearby construction site, the soldiers beat back the flames. When Dakin and the Sheppard family returned home, hoping to salvage whatever they could from the ruins, they were delighted to find the house sitting unscathed at the top of the hill. It was surrounded by a sea of ashes.

The Appraiser's Building and the Montgomery Block were a success story as well. On Friday, for a third time, fire threatened—this time from the north as it rushed down Telegraph Hill through blocks of wooden shacks.

Some of the soldiers, firefighters, and civilians in the Montgomery Block had been battling flames in the area since Wednesday. Many were civilians employed by the A. P. Hotaling liquor company. Their primary mission was to save the whiskey barrels they had rolled into a previously burned area on Wednesday, in anticipation of the military dynamiting their warehouse (which it never did). The weary men had already fought fires from the south on Wednesday and from the west on Thursday. When fire approached once more, this time from the north, the men despaired. But just as the situation appeared hopeless, the wind direction changed and began blowing from the southeast, holding up the fire's progress. The men rallied and teamed up with the soldiers to try to save the block once again.

Lacking water, the men ingeniously substituted another kind of liquid. Using wine pumps, they drained nearby sewers, and they siphoned saltwater seepage that had collected in a construction excavation. The mixture of foul-smelling sewage and seepage was pumped into some barrels, then poured into buckets and pails for a bucket brigade. Edward Lind, a Hotaling employee, wrote this account of the fight to save the Montgomery Block. It was published in a local journal, the *Argonaut,* in 1926:

> The old Eiffel Tower restaurant building . . . was in full blaze, and the sparks from this fire threatened at any moment to start another blaze in the old lodging house across the street on the southeast corner, which was part of our block. If that happened we knew we were done for.
>
> The hose we had been using so successfully all through the night had been taken away, or burnt by the fire on Telegraph Hill, and we had only our buckets to depend on. These had to be passed in through

the lodging house door and up the winding stairway to the attic, and then up a rickety ladder through a small manhole to the roof, and scattered over the exposed woodwork or on live sparks as they fell. . . .

One side of Jackson Street was a roaring fury of flame, with walls toppling and smoke choking people. Along the other side we had to keep the buckets going no matter how we blistered or smarted. On the roof of the lodging house it felt like a barbecue. The buckets could not come quick enough, and the evil-smelling stuff made a steam that was suffocating as it evaporated on the roasting woodwork.

Finally the Eiffel Tower house collapsed. Our side of the street was still unscathed, and danger from that source was ended.

✦   ✦   ✦

The fire in the Mission District raged all day Friday. The National Guard, which had arrived in the city late Wednesday to assist with the disaster, attempted several times to use dynamite to check the flames' steady southward progress. Unfortunately, the dynamite kept sparking additional blazes, and the men continually had to fall back. Finally firefighters and members of the National Guard developed a plan. To prevent further westward advance, they would create a firebreak at Dolores Street, a particularly wide road with a park between 18th and 20th Streets. To stop the fire from moving further south, they would create a firebreak along seven blocks of 20th Street, between Dolores and Howard Streets.

Fortified by the arrival of an experienced navy dynamite squad, the National Guard soldiers dynamited an expanse along Dolores Street in the west and along Howard Street to the east. This was the first successful use of dynamite in the fight against the South of Market fire, most likely because the dynamite was handled by experienced people and used far enough in advance of the flames to make the firebreak effective. Plus, enough water was available, from cisterns and pooled water from a broken water main at Howard Street, to contain the small fires that sprang up when the dynamite was set off.

To the south, between Dolores and Howard Streets, soldiers, civilians, and firefighters worked together to demolish structures on the north side of 20th Street. They used dynamite to blow large structures apart, and smaller structures were pulled down by hand.

The men's efforts received a boost when water was discovered on 20th Street. Accounts differ as to whether the source was a working hydrant, a cistern, or a private well. However, it was located at the top of a hill so steep that the exhausted horses could not drag the fire engine there. Hundreds of refugees, who were camped out in nearby Mission Dolores Park, rushed to help. Together they successfully pushed the engine up the hill.

When the blaze finally roared toward them, the firefighters were stunned by its intensity. Large sparks and firebrands preceded it, blowing across the firebreaks and threatening to ignite structures across the streets. Poisonous gasses emanated from the flames as well, rolling invisibly among the volunteers and knocking them over. In response, defiant firefighters perched on rooftops with wet sacks, beating out sparks. On the ground more volunteers huddled beneath doors that had been wrested from buildings for use as fire shields. Firefighters with damp sacks dashed forward to beat out the flames for a few minutes, until the heat became overpowering. Then they retreated and other volunteers moved forward to take their places.

Through the heroic efforts of civilians, soldiers, and city firefighters in the Mission District, the massive blaze

the inferno continued to rage, moving inexorably southeast. At last, the extraordinary efforts of these persistent
civilian and navy firefighters succeeded, and at Pier 27,
they contained the blaze. It was Saturday morning.
After three long, terrible days, the Great Fire of 1906
was finally over.

Controversy and the Military

Many residents of earthquake-stricken San Francisco incorrectly believed that martial law had been proclaimed by President Theodore Roosevelt immediately following the earthquake. Whether legal or not, the military presence in the devastated city ensured much-needed assistance in firefighting, crowd control, and law enforcement efforts.

6

B oth during and after the fire, San Franciscans were not sure how they felt about the presence of the military in their devastated city. The controversy over whether or not military groups had a positive or negative effect on the city's handling of the crisis raged on for decades. It has never been settled. On the one hand, the military's presence reassured citizens that order would be kept in spite of the destruction sweeping the city. On the other hand, many citizens were outraged by the oppressive treatment they and their neighbors received from the soldiers.

Part of the difficulty of assigning blame—or praise—for any military group's actions was the vast number of different military and quasi-military groups roaming the streets of San Francisco. Among the armed groups vested with varying degrees of authority were the police, army,

71

navy, marines, National Guard, University of California Berkeley Cadet Corps, and "special police" (civilians issued stars and special passes by Mayor Schmitz and granted the right to carry firearms). While actions of the army, navy, marines, and Cadet Corps were often praised, the conduct of members of the National Guard and the special police seemed to bear the brunt of the criticism. Still, it was difficult for citizens to know which soldiers belonged to which group. To most San Franciscans, a uniform meant "soldier," and that was classification enough.

Among the soldiers' tasks were evacuating residents from the path of the flames and keeping civilians out of the fire zone, enforced by establishing "fire lines" that civilians were forbidden to cross. Although the soldiers' orders were issued with civilian safety in mind, some members of the military were overly aggressive in carrying out their instructions. Many eyewitnesses reported that soldiers drove people from their homes and businesses hours before the flames closed in, forcing residents to flee at bayonet point without having the opportunity to save cherished possessions or crucial business records.

Arnold Genthe, a well-known photographer who snapped several of the most famous photographs of the earthquake and fire, had a run-in with a hostile soldier when he attempted to salvage some of his possessions from his studio:

> I hurried up Sutter Street to find a militiaman guarding the entrance of my studio.
>
> "You can't get in here," he said, handling his rifle in an unpleasant manner.
>
> "But it's my home," I said.
>
> "I don't care whether it is or not. Orders are to clear all houses on the block. If you don't do as I say, I shoot, see?"

There were rumors that some of the militia, drunk with liquor and power, had been shooting people. I did not want to argue with him, but I did want to get inside, with the hope that I might save a few of my things.

Genthe gained entrance to his apartment by giving the soldier a bottle of whiskey. However, it wasn't long before the militiaman resumed his hostile attitude. Genthe's account continues, "When my militia friend had absorbed enough of his bottle, he pushed me through the door, saying, 'Now you have got to get out of here or I'll have to shoot you, see?'" Genthe left his studio and quietly watched with his neighbors as his home was destroyed by dynamite.

Many businessmen particularly resented being forced to abandon fire-resistant buildings that they were certain could have been saved with the help of their employees.

Large crowds gather to watch firefighting efforts. Curiosity seekers were kept from getting too close to the flames by soldiers who kept them behind "fire lines." Some people would claim that members of the military were too aggressive in carrying out these orders.

William E. Keller, president of Globe Flour Mill, located on Montgomery Street, complained bitterly of the soldiers' rigid, thoughtless enforcement of their orders. He wrote the following account:

> On Friday afternoon, as the flames approached, we got ten of our men, and were confident of success in saving the mill. At four o'clock in the afternoon, soldiers appeared and ordered us out, threatening to shoot if we did not go. Arguments and explanations were of no avail. We were ordered to go or be shot. We left the building, and late at night, after being exposed for many hours to the heat of burning lumber yards to the north and east, windows in the east front at length broke, and bins of wheat thus directly exposed to the heat, were ignited. There is of course no doubt whatsoever that one man could have saved the structure had he been permitted to remain. Our loss was $220,000.

In a report written by lawyer Frank Hittell, he accused the military of another type of injustice: enforcing fire lines so strictly that it prevented volunteers from helping the exhausted and overworked firefighters:

> Late on Wednesday . . . a fireman approached a crowd of men who were being kept back by the military, and asked for volunteers. So thoroughly cowed were the citizens by the soldiers that no one responded, although I knew that every man of them was willing to help. I went forward and was stopped by a soldier who ordered me back. I refused to go back, informed him that I was responding to the call of a fireman for volunteers, and finally, after prolonged argument, was permitted to pass.

The firemen were surprised to find only one volunteer. When Hittell explained that the men were afraid to

defy the soldiers, the firefighters asked him to go back and try to get more volunteers through the fire lines. Although Hittell had no trouble finding 20 volunteers, the soldiers steadfastly refused to let the men pass. It was not until the firemen returned and begged the soldiers to relent that the volunteers were finally allowed through.

Another issue that generated much controversy about the military was, of course, its implementation of Schmitz's order to shoot looters. In addition to resulting in the deaths of civilians, the troops' fanatical dedication to stamping out looting sometimes prevented citizens from taking much-needed food and supplies from stores that were sure to burn. After the fire General Funston denied that there had been any widespread killing during

San Francisco resident Arnold Genthe, considered the father of American photography, documented scenes such as this view of the fire from earthquake-ravaged Sacramento Street. Much of Genthe's other work was lost when his photography studio was dynamited to create a firebreak.

the military occupation. "There was no necessity for the regular troops to shoot anybody and there is no well-authenticated case of a single person having been killed by regular troops," he would later announce. "Two men were shot by the state troops under circumstances with which I am not familiar . . . and one prominent citizen was ruthlessly slain by self-constituted vigilantes."

However, this assertion conflicts with eyewitness reports. Many observers reported seeing people shot or bayoneted; others reported seeing corpses lying in the street, labeled with placards reading "Looter." Some claimed that citizens were killed by the soldiers for offenses such as profiteering (charging outrageous prices for food and supplies) or refusing to work with the soldiers or firemen when ordered to do so. The number of citizens killed by military groups will never be known, since most bodies and physical evidence were incinerated in the firestorm.

In addition to the controversy over the shoot-to-kill order, at some point soldiers reinterpreted the military's original orders to close down all liquor-selling establishments. The troops began to break into saloons and other establishments and dump the liquor stocks into the sewers. This aggressive behavior frightened many citizens, especially since some of the seized liquor found its way into a few soldiers' mouths.

All of this military strong-arming lent support to the widespread, but erroneous, assumption that the city was under martial law. This was understandable; policemen were few and far between, and the only law enforcement agencies seemed to be the army, the National Guard, and other military groups. Few people argued points of law with soldiers armed with rifles and bayonets, especially since the military was rumored to be shooting looters and other offenders on sight.

The newspapers contributed to this perception of military rule as well. On the morning of Thursday, April 18, three of San Francisco's newspapers—the *Call,* the *Chronicle,* and the *Examiner*—put aside their differences long enough to produce a joint issue on the presses of the *Oakland Tribune.* This four-page paper was distributed free of charge throughout the burning city. Its report on the earthquake and fiery aftermath contained several erroneous assertions, including one that made the rumors of martial law seem fact: "At nine o'clock, under a special message from President [Theodore] Roosevelt, the city was placed under martial law." In fact, there had been no such message from the president.

Early Wednesday morning General Funston had informed Mayor Schmitz that he intended at all times to consult with civilian authorities about planned military actions. Although this consultation was occasionally lacking, Funston never actively tried to seize full control of the city. Mayor Schmitz, although annoyed by the autocratic behavior of General Funston and his troops, generally allowed Funston to do as he saw fit. Schmitz realized that the military presence in the days immediately following the earthquake was the most effective means of preventing chaos from sweeping the city. Without soldiers the city may well have descended into violence and chaos.

In addition, the manpower the military provided was desperately needed. The navy, in particular, under the command of Lieutenant Frederick Freedman, had contributed immensely in both battling the fires and keeping order along the waterfront. In fact, after the first day of the fire, the navy had assumed almost sole responsibility for harbor firefighting and patrolling. Midshipman John E. Pond, commander of the fire tug *Active,* commented on the persistent efforts that he and his navy compatriots

(continued on p. 80)

LIEUTENANT FREDERICK FREEMAN

Many San Franciscans appreciated the extensive firefighting and rescue efforts performed by members of the military during the disaster. But the extent of the navy's contributions was not really known until a report by the commanding officer, Lieutenant Frederick Freeman, was discovered in the National Archives in Washington, D.C., and declassified in the 1980s.

The classified status of Freeman's report is puzzling. The National Archives declared that it was a mistake. Whatever the reason, the classified status prevented anyone from knowing of the pivotal role that Lieutenant Freeman had played in the fight against the fire caused by the San Francisco earthquake of 1906.

Freeman seems to have been everywhere during the crisis. Almost all of the areas that were rescued along the waterfront, in addition to a few inland locations, owed their continued existence at least in part to Lieutenant Freeman and his men.

After arriving on the destroyer *Preble* (a floating hospital) on the morning of Wednesday, April 18, Freeman immediately got to work. He sent a medical team ashore to help the injured and directed the fireboats *Leslie* and *Active* to assist the city fire department. By evening, squads of firefighting sailors that had been sent to the South of Market area saved buildings along the waterfront from Howard Street south to Townsend Street.

Next, with the *Leslie*, Freeman orchestrated the delivery of water to firefighters defending the Southern Pacific freight sheds and rail yards at Eighth and Townsend Streets. That fire was declared under control at 2:30 A.M. Thursday morning. Later that morning, Freeman assumed control of the the waterfront area, detailing men to patrol the area to prevent looting, close saloons, and help refugees.

On Thursday afternoon and evening, Freeman turned his attention inland. He ran a mile-long line of hose from the San Francisco Bay to the Montgomery Block. In his report, he commends his men for doing their best work there:

> The men of my command at this point showed the greatest daring and perseverance, going to the tops of buildings and extinguishing fires in cornices and windows, going through large buildings before the fire reached them and

The clock tower of the Ferry Building can barely be seen through the smoke enveloping the burning San Francisco waterfront. The final battle against the fire took place north of here, as Lieutenant Freeman directed naval firefighters in a desperate battle to stop the flames from devastating all the city's warehouses and piers.

tearing down all inflammable material, such as curtains, awnings, etc., and I have no doubt that this section of the city was saved entirely by their efforts.

Friday afternoon found Freeman fighting the fire on Telegraph Hill. He and Lieutenant Brewster of the marines were hoping to prevent the blaze from reaching the nearby waterfront by holding the fire at bay with streams of water from the *Active*. But then the wind changed to the northwest, driving the fire directly on them. To save their lives, Freeman and his men had to hurriedly evacuate the area, leaving hundreds of feet of hose to the flames.

Freeman and his men spent the remaining hours of the fire on board the Leslie and the *Active*, furiously pouring water on the flames along the waterfront in hopes of saving as many docks and warehouses as possible. At times the men labored in an inferno as burning cinders showered the decks of the fireboats.

Early Saturday morning the fireboats, in conjunction with firefighters working on the shore, finally managed to bring the fire at the waterfront under control. Freeman and his men had spent three straight days on duty. Their heroic efforts enabled much of the waterfront to escape destruction, ensuring the economic survival of San Francisco.

Thousands were left without food and shelter following the earthquake and fire. Once the flames were out, members of the military and law enforcement turned their efforts to helping distribute food to the hungry crowds. Here, officers hand out flour rations to homeless San Franciscans.

(continued from p. 77)

made in fighting the blaze:

> From that Wednesday morning until the fire was under control the following Saturday, April 21, we worked almost steadily with little rest. The city firemen worked with us all of the first day and night. After that very few of them were to be seen in the waterfront district. Many of them left to look after their own families, while our men, most of whom had no kin in the city, stuck to their posts until they almost collapsed.

The military also played an important role after the fire had run its course. As the most organized group in the city, the army was best prepared to tackle the immense task of caring for hundreds of thousands of refugees. Soldiers organized the initial relief efforts at Golden Gate Park and the Presidio. The soldiers didn't entirely escape criticism during the months after the fire, however. Residents complained about the military's practice of forcing able-bodied men to clear rubble from the streets. This forced-labor operation went on for several weeks, until residents' mounting complaints forced Mayor Schmitz and Governor Pardee to order an end to it.

Still, by the time the regular army, the last military group to withdraw from San Francisco, left on July 1, 1906, the soldiers were being lauded for their work. Americans considered General Funston a local—even national—hero.

No one will ever be able to say with certainty if General Funston made the correct decision when he ordered in his troops in response to the great disaster. It is certain that Schmitz's order to shoot looters was illegal and should not have been carried out. In addition, General Funston and his subordinates, as well as the officers of the other military groups on duty in the city, share the blame for failing to rein in the troops who abused their authority. But considering the unprecedented devastation that the earthquake and fire wreaked on the city, the military's presence was probably necessary and appropriate.

"We Have No City, but Lots of Hope"

Looking west on Market Street from the Ferry Building. Although more than one half of the city lay in ruins after the earthquake and fire, the city's residents proved resilient in their efforts to begin rebuilding.

O n Saturday evening, April 21, 1906, rain began to fall in San Francisco. It drenched the hundreds of thousands of homeless refugees in San Francisco's parks. Steam rose from the wreckage of what had been the West's greatest city, "the American Paris," whose ashes still glowed from the quenched inferno.

Now the enormity of the destruction began to sink into the hearts and minds of San Francisco's citizens. More than 4.7 square miles of the city had been destroyed, leaving 225,000 people homeless—over half the city's population of 400,000. Approximately 500 city blocks and over 28,000 buildings had been reduced to rubble or gutted shells. The damage would run to $400 million in 1906 dollars—a sum so vast it was almost incomprehensible at the time.

And then there was the death toll. The U.S. Army would place the number of casualties from 450 to 500. Later estimates would raise it to approximately 700. Accurate body counts were impossible to get. The South of Market district, one of the city's most crowded areas, had been particularly hard hit. Hundreds of people trapped in earthquake-ravaged buildings had perished in the fast-moving flames. The intense heat of the inferno, which reached temperatures as high as 2,700 degrees Fahrenheit, ensured that no forensic evidence survived the flames. Citizens would never know if missing acquaintances had perished in the disaster or merely fled the city, never to return.

The two estimates of approximately 500 dead and 700 dead were cited until the 1990s, when Gladys Hansen, the curator of the Museum of San Francisco and the former archivist for the city and county of San Francisco, finished an exhaustive study of the city's records. In addition to counting those killed directly by the earthquake and fire, Hansen also included deaths from suicide and disease resulting from living in refugee camps. She determined that the actual death toll from the disaster was more than 3,000 persons.

This number represented only a small fraction of the San Franciscans affected by the earthquake and the three-day fire. The disaster had injured thousands and left hundreds of thousands homeless. Shortly after the quake as many as 300,000 people were sleeping outdoors. Many of them were not actually homeless. Some residents camping out in the parks lived in homes that had survived the earthquake and fire unscathed, but they were too afraid of the aftershocks to sleep inside.

The number of refugees in the relief camps soon began to dwindle as many left the city. The Southern Pacific railroad helped carry many of them; the railroad

would eventually transport more than 225,000 refugees out of San Francisco, all at its own cost. Many San Franciscans who left would ultimately return when the city was rebuilt. In the meantime, families that remained doubled up in surviving homes, and large homes were converted into apartments and rooming houses.

Although life in the refugee camps was far from comfortable, there were no food or water shortages in San Francisco after the fire was over. Organized relief efforts had begun on the day of the disaster—the first train carrying supplies arrived just 19 hours after the quake struck. Cities all over the United States swung into action as soon as the dire situation in San Francisco was publicized. So much food was sent before distribution was organized that some of it ended up rotting on docks and in railway depots.

San Francisco also received vast sums of money

Military leaders and Red Cross officials quickly established facilities to supply hot food to the thousands of people left homeless in the wake of the earthquake and subsequent fire.

Even in homes that had managed to survive both the earthquake and fire, no cooking was allowed inside until city officials ensured that stoves and chimneys would not spark new blazes. Families living in temporary housing set up their own outdoor kitchens as well.

donated to relief by cities and towns all over the United States. Even foreign nations donated money to the cause, although President Theodore Roosevelt refused their assistance. Within a day of the quake, Congress had appropriated $1 million for San Francisco's relief. The city would ultimately receive a total of $9 million in relief funds.

President Roosevelt, concerned about allowing disaster relief money to fall into the hands of San Francisco's corrupt city government, designated the Red Cross as the sole handler of these funds. He appointed Dr. Edward Devine to head the organization and handle relief operations.

The newly reorganized agency played a huge role in relief in the days immediately after the fire. Coordinating its efforts with those of the army and the National Guard, the Red Cross distributed food, water, and basic necessities—such as clothing and bedding—at relief camps sprinkled throughout the city.

To distribute funds the Red Cross and the San Francisco Relief Committee established special committees, which worked hard to ensure that funds went to the most needy and those most able to make good use of the money. The committees distributed the bulk of the money in the form of small grants to be used to start or restart small businesses.

Before the earthquake the Red Cross had been a small organization that many people didn't even think was necessary. They thought that in times of crisis the local residents could handle their own problems. The San Francisco earthquake and fire justified the need for an agency like the Red Cross. The disaster relief mission was the largest the Red Cross had yet undertaken. As a result of its work in San Francisco, the organization gained a great deal of respect and rose to national prominence. Red Cross relief efforts served to heighten the organization's name recognition in the United States and prepare it for the significant role it would play in military and civilian relief in World War I.

For weeks following the disaster, food and water were available only through bread lines. Rich and poor alike stood patiently, sometimes for hours, waiting for their share. Some people actually enjoyed the feeling that they were linked to their neighbors in a great brotherhood of suffering and survival. In her article for the April 29, 1906, *San Francisco Bulletin,* writer Pauline Jacobson described how it felt to be an earthquake and fire refugee: "Most of us . . . have run the whole gamut of human emotions from glad to sad and back again, but underneath it all a new note is struck, a quiet bubbling joy is felt. It is that note that makes all our loss worth the while. It is the note of a millennial good fellowship. . . . Everybody [is] your friend and you in turn [are] everybody's friend."

For the most part, people in the refugee camps were cheerful. Makeshift cafés sprang up, made from boxes and tin. Some provoked laughs with amusing inscriptions. One proverb inscribed in chalk on a café read "Eat, drink and be merry, for tomorrow we may have to go to Oakland." Poems were widely circulated, too, such as this one:

> The cow is in the hammock,
> The cat is in the lake,
> The baby in the garbage can,
> What difference does it make?
> There is no water, and still less soap.
> We have no city, but lots of hope.

Businesses burned out of downtown also joined in. One lawyer hung a sign on his ruined office building that said he had "moved because the elevators were not running." Another sign placed on a pile of rubble said, "Forced to move on account of alterations on April 18th."

In spite of all this good humor, there were some problems in the refugee camps. The one that worried relief organizers the most was sanitation. Red Cross workers instructed citizens to boil all water before drinking it, and encouraged them to use sanitation trenches and properly dispose of their garbage. Despite the effort made to impose sanitation rules on the camps, some outbreaks of smallpox and typhoid did occur. Luckily, these diseases were contained before widespread epidemics could take hold. Sanitary conditions eventually improved, and outbreaks of disease became rarer. The only significant exception was an outbreak of bubonic plague in May 1907 that killed 77 people.

San Franciscans immediately jumped into the rebuilding process, and by the fall of 1906, only 17,000 refugees

Residents gather outside the U.S. Post Office, anxiously waiting for letters. The Post Office Building was one of the few structures in the South of Market area still standing after the disaster. The Friday after the quake, while fire still raged in the city, the government agency was providing service—mail could be sent free of charge, and letters could be written on anything, as long as the surface was flat.

remained in the relief camps. So as not to foster dependence, camp authorities encouraged the remaining citizens to find work, leave the camps, and pay for their food as soon as they could. Before winter, most tents had been replaced by two- or three-room cottages, dubbed "refugee shacks," built for the 11,000 citizens still homeless. The cottages and camps were all gone by the end of the summer of 1908. Residents of refugee shacks were encouraged to purchase building lots, and their cottages were then moved to these lots. As the decades passed, the refugee shacks would be altered and added onto until they became completely unrecognizable.

As for those whose homes were lucky enough to escape destruction by earthquake and flames, their everyday lives were transformed as well. Soldiers were everywhere. No gas, electricity, running water, or sewer service was available for weeks, and the soldiers enforced a strict lights-out curfew at 7 P.M. The streets of San Francisco were transformed by thousands of makeshift outdoor stoves. No one in San Francisco was allowed to cook indoors until chimneys had been inspected and pronounced safe. The repair and inspection process took months.

Just as the rebuilding of the city began within a few days, so did the process of collecting on fire insurance policies. In the early 1900s, insurance was a fairly new industry, and a poorly regulated one. Many people did not have insurance, and those who did often did not have enough.

Insured San Franciscans soon discovered that not all insurance companies were equal. There were significant differences between insurance companies in their handling of the claims. Unfortunately, many more companies acted dishonorably than honorably. Only a handful of companies paid immediately and in full.

Twelve insurance companies failed as a result of their losses. Most paid their customers only a portion of the promised policy award, withholding amounts from 2 to 25 percent. Company officials excused their actions, pointing out that earthquake damage was excluded from coverage. Since it was nearly impossible to determine how much damage was caused by the fire and how much by the earthquake, they claimed to be justified in reducing damage awards. The worst offenders were three German companies and an Austrian company that defaulted completely and withdrew from doing business in the United States to avoid punishment.

Still, in spite of problems, the relief donations and

money collected from the insurance companies seemed to be enough to set San Francisco immediately to rebuilding. The survival of the U.S. Mint helped ease the city's early financial recovery, for it was the only significant source of cash in the entire area. Although money was still in bank vaults throughout the city, no one could get to it yet.

Bank officials knew they had to wait before opening their vaults. Two years earlier, when a major fire struck the city of Baltimore, Maryland, bank officers there had swung open their sizzling-hot vaults immediately after the fire. The sudden introduction of oxygen into the still superheated vaults had caused their currency and papers to burst into flame. It would be several weeks before the vaults in the San Francisco banks had cooled enough for officials to finally open them. Luckily, no banks lost any assets to fire.

The saving of the U.S. Post Office building was another key factor in San Francisco's recovery. With the telephone and telegraph systems down, businesses could still use the postal service to resume communication with out-of-town business partners. Residents could inform friends and relatives around the country that they were all right—and that they needed money.

The post office began collecting mail again on Friday, April 20, even before the fire was out. Although the earthquake had damaged the building heavily, not a single piece of mail in the post office's possession on Wednesday had been lost to the quake or the flames. During the first few weeks following the disaster, the post office accepted, even without a stamp, letters written on anything flat enough to be reasonably mailed. This included everything from wooden roof shingles to men's detachable collars. Paper might have been rare, but written communication was still possible.

Rebuilding from the Ashes

In some streets, debris and rubble were removed by railcars, which ran on specially installed tracks. In other areas horse-drawn carts and wagons helped workers clear wreckage from the roads. Cleanup of the city would not end until the spring of the following year.

Everything the devastated city of San Francisco needed for a quick recovery was at hand: The U.S. Mint provided a ready source of cash until the banks could recover, and mechanisms for receiving goods were in place. Ships could deliver supplies to the numerous wharves that had been saved along the waterfront, and the Southern Pacific railroad's tracks were intact.

City leaders debated whether to improve the city's layout while rebuilding. The existing streets of San Francisco had been developed as a basic grid, with no regard for beauty or the contours of its many hills. An ambitious blueprint for remodeling the city already existed—in 1905 the famous architect Daniel H. Burnham had drawn up a plan that called for cutting new streets and creating new plazas and parks.

Another issue in rebuilding the city, to the prejudiced white majority, was the proposed relocation of Chinatown. East of Russian Hill and north of Nob Hill, Chinatown took up 16 blocks of desirable real estate. The Committee of Fifty set up a group to discuss this resettlement issue. However, while the Committee on Relocating the Chinese debated the proper location for a new Chinatown, the Chinese quietly began rebuilding. Those involved in the push to relocate the Chinese had forgotten that many Chinatown residents actually owned a good portion of the property in that part of the city and legally could not be prevented from resettling there. Ironically, the new Chinatown would grow to become a key component of the new San Francisco, eventually developing into one of the city's main attractions.

Just as the plan to relocate the Chinese met with failure, so did the attempt to implement the Burnham plan. In order to maintain its position as the premier trading port of the West, San Francisco had to rebuild quickly. There was no time to raise funding for new streets or to fight court battles with the property owners displaced by the new plan. So the Burnham design was mostly ignored, and the city was rebuilt on its original grid.

San Francisco did have a plan beyond merely rebuilding, however. Before the quake struck, the city had been vying to host the Panama–Pacific International Exposition in 1915, a world's fair that would celebrate the 1914 opening of the Panama Canal. The newly built canal would connect the Atlantic and Pacific Oceans, reducing ship travel distance between America's east and west coasts by about 7,000 miles. Construction of the Panama Canal had begun in 1907. When it opened, whichever city was the primary port in the West could expect to see a big boost in business. San Francisco recognized that it had to rebuild quickly to retain its status as a premier trading center.

Not long after the fire was quenched, the city put the Panama–Pacific International Exposition plans back into motion. City leaders felt hosting the event would be an excellent way of putting the disaster behind them and proving to the world how quickly and fully their city had recovered. Accordingly, an area of the bay shoreline to the north, next to Fort Mason, was filled in with rubble from the fire, to create new land on which to stage the exposition. In 1911 the city won the right to hold the fair, which it successfully hosted four years later.

The exposition planners were not the only San Franciscans with an eye toward public relations. Business groups all over the city wanted to emphasize San Francisco's recovery from its tragedy. They wanted to be certain that people would continue to invest, build, live, and do business in San Francisco.

Members of the Building Committee supervise cleanup efforts. In the distance can be seen smoke rising from dynamited buildings deemed too unsafe to repair.

The biggest obstacle to the public's perception of the safety of San Francisco, city leaders realized, was the earthquake, not the fire. Major cities were expected to have fires from time to time. But earthquakes were poorly understood and terrifying. San Francisco's businessmen were determined to minimize information about earthquake damage and instead place the blame for most of the destruction on the fire. Accordingly, within a few years most of San Francisco's residents were referring to the catastrophe as the Great Fire rather than as the Great Earthquake.

MAYOR SCHMITZ AND ABE RUEF

Just after the disaster, many San Franciscans considered Mayor Schmitz a hero. They saw him as a true leader, unafraid to make difficult decisions or take quick action during the crisis. But it wasn't long before Mayor Schmitz and his mentor, political boss Abe Ruef, returned to their corrupt ways.

Soon after the crisis ended, San Francisco mayor Eugene Schmitz (left) and political boss Abe Ruef began lining their pockets with bribes and engaging once more in political graft.

No one could rival the Southern Pacific Railroad at the public relations game. Eager to bring business back to its hub city, the railroad carefully sanitized discussions of the disaster. It sponsored a local periodical, *Sunset Magazine,* featuring articles that downplayed the earthquake, played up the fire, and painted a promising picture of San Francisco's cheerful and rapid recovery from the disaster. In later years historians would use *Sunset Magazine* as a primary source. In that way the Southern Pacific's whitewashed version of the disaster came to be considered gospel truth.

After the earthquake the Home Telephone Company, which had paid Ruef significant "fees," was awarded the contract for telephone service, although the other phone companies had not even known that the city was soliciting bids. Another firm that paid hefty "fees" to Ruef—the United Railroads Company—was allowed to construct overhead cables for a new trolley system, despite the opposition of most citizens, who preferred the previous system, based on underground cables.

Unfortunately for Ruef and Schmitz, their enemies, some of San Francisco's wealthiest and most influential citizens, soon launched and bankrolled an investigation into city government corruption. As soon as the chaos following the earthquake and fire had died down, investigators unearthed ample evidence of wrongdoing, and Ruef and Schmitz were indicted in the fall of 1906.

Abe Ruef faced the more serious charges. In an attempt to reduce his sentence, he incriminated Mayor Schmitz, who in June 1907 was sentenced to five years at San Quentin prison. Ruef was sentenced to 14 years at San Quentin.

Schmitz, still popular with his former constituents, served only seven months of his term—all of it in the county jail. His conviction was overturned by the California State Court of Appeals, and he was set free. Years after his acquittal, Schmitz actually returned to public life. Although a subsequent mayoral bid proved unsuccessful, Schmitz was twice elected to the city's board of supervisors. Apparently his native city had forgiven him.

As for Abe Ruef, he served only four and a half years of his term before being released on parole. However, he was never allowed to resume his law practice, and in 1936 the great political boss died penniless.

One of the few buildings in the Mission District that withstood the flames, the U.S. Mint, nicknamed the Granite Lady, stands alone in a sea of debris. The survival of the Mint ensured a ready supply of currency needed to help restart businesses.

This kind of maneuvering contributed to an already pervasive problem that would plague all future accounts of and investigations into the earthquake and fire: it was impossible to discern the truth. Details on the number of casualties, movement of the fire, behavior of the military, and other aspects of the disaster vary slightly in all written accounts, depending on the version.

Some of the information that appears in books about the earthquake and fire is completely false. As soon as the flames died, writers were at work composing lurid accounts of the disaster for publication in dime novels—melodramatic stories that were popular with the American public at the time. These dime novels were based on spurious newspaper reports and uncorroborated tales from "eyewitnesses" who had fled the city.

One tale that gained widespread circulation was about an attempt to rob the U.S. Mint, during which 14 men were shot and killed by the soldiers guarding the facility. Although the Mint had been guarded during the fire, such an attack never took place. Another earthquake story that circulated claimed "ghouls" had looted the dead by cutting or biting off their ears and fingers to steal earrings and rings. None of these tales was ever corroborated.

The military's shooting of looters was played up as well. Although facts indicate that some civilians were indeed killed by various military groups, it is highly unlikely that the death toll from military shootings and bayonetings ever reached the hundreds proclaimed by some newspapers and books.

Newspaper accounts were as bad as those in the dime novels. In their desire to scoop one another, newspapers across the country published phony, dramatic stories about deaths, shootings, riots, and other mayhem resulting from the earthquake. Photographs that were faked to heighten quake or fire damage often accompanied the phony stories.

Even the newspapers that intended to print the facts often published erroneous information because it was so hard to learn the truth. While the fires were raging, local reporters had not been allowed to cross the fire lines to talk with the firefighters. During the crisis reporters from other cities had been kept out of San Francisco by an order from General Funston that prohibited anyone from entering the city. And eyewitnesses fleeing for their lives often gave conflicting accounts of the chaotic events in the rubble-filled, smoke-obscured streets.

When writing their accounts of the San Francisco earthquake, later historians turned to newspaper and magazine articles and to authentic "rare" books from the time. Unfortunately, the rare books of today are the dime novels of yesterday. Some of the lies originally invented to sell books to the American public eventually found their way into scholarly discussions of the quake.

None of the unanswered questions or unresolved controversies about the biggest disaster ever to hit an American city are likely to be resolved. Few, if any, earthquake survivors remain alive, and no forensic evidence remains.

Perhaps it doesn't matter. Because even though the record of the disaster is blurry, San Francisco achieved its goal: within three years the city was rebuilt, and it regained its status as the key American port on the Pacific Ocean.

Reforms, Lessons Not Learned, and the 1989 Earthquake

Still a new invention in 1906 America, the automobile proved its usefulness in communication, evacuation, and firefighting efforts (including carrying supplies of dynamite to firebreak areas). After the disaster, city officials purchased several vehicles for administrative, fire department, and law enforcement use.

T he almost complete devastation of San Francisco gave its scientists, citizens, and civic leaders a unique opportunity to learn from the disaster and make improvements that would help prevent similar destruction in future earthquakes. Unfortunately, San Francisco, for the most part, squandered this opportunity. Still, in spite of their reluctance to make good use of the knowledge gained from the earthquake and fire, San Franciscans did make some positive changes to improve their future.

Soon after the disaster Governor George C. Pardee appointed a scientific commission to investigate the earthquake. The commission included professors from California's most prestigious universities, as well as experts from the U.S. Geological Survey, the government agency responsible for studying the earth's structure and managing the nation's mineral resources. Despite the fact that the commission received no state funding and that the public-relations-sensitive business and civic communities discouraged its efforts, it delivered a report that set the standard for all future earthquake studies.

This 1908 report, funded by the Carnegie Institute of Washington, is called the Lawson Report, for University of California professor Andrew Lawson, the head of Governor Pardee's commission. The group and its report spawned the creation of the Seismological Society of America and transformed seismology from a fringe science to a mainstream and widely studied one. Release of the Lawson Report marked the beginning of modern seismology in the United States.

One of the most important parts of the report was Professor Henry Fielding Reid's elastic-rebound theory, which gives a basic explanation of the mechanism of earthquakes. Professor Reid's theory still remains valid today, despite the fact that in 1908 knowledge of the movement of the earth's crust, or plate tectonics, was still decades in the future.

The report also contains detailed maps of the San Andreas Fault and other lesser fault lines in the Bay Area, as well as maps showing the 1906 earthquake's intensity by location. These intensity maps, which indicate the stability of the underlying soil throughout the Bay Area, are used today in seismic risk assessment for buildings. Unfortunately, the scientists' recommendations in 1908 regarding unstable land had little effect on rebuilding strategies. In their rush to rebuild the city, San Franciscans just built in the same spots, even where the soil had become unstable enough to liquefy.

Still, San Franciscans did learn some lessons from the disaster. In keeping with their campaign to suppress discussion of the earthquake and blame most of the

Spurred by their desire to quickly rebuild in order to host the Panama–Pacific International Exposition in 1915, city administrators made decisions that would prove to be disastrous to future generations—building structures such as this Exposition pavilion on land created by dumping earthquake debris and rubble.

destruction on the fire, they concentrated their reform efforts on the city's water supply. They wanted to minimize the risk of another citywide conflagration occurring, even if a future earthquake should damage the pipes leading to the main reservoirs. Accordingly, the fire department and the city developed and built a backup water system, called the *high-pressure water system,* or the auxiliary water supply system. One multimillion-gallon reservoir and two half-million-gallon tanks were built within the city limits, at high elevations so gravity would be the primary provider of water pressure.

The city also built two saltwater pumping stations near the bay. These could pump water into the high-pressure water system in case mains to the hilltop reservoirs were broken. City engineers built several pipes that led to the waterfront, where, if all else failed, the city's two fireboats could hook into the high-pressure water system and pump salt water directly into it.

Water main pipes were designed so that just a few valves could turn off the water supply to various areas of the city. That way the city would be able to shut off water service to heavily damaged areas, minimizing the risk of losing water through broken pipes and valves. Finally, the fire department restored many of the existing water cisterns located throughout the city, and added 85 new ones.

Based on its experiences during the quake, the police department made it a priority to purchase automobiles. Members of law enforcement realized these autos would help them effectively protect public safety. Overall, the disaster served as the beginning of the Bay Area's love affair with the automobile. Before the earthquake, autos were considered frivolous toys. But during the quake the usual mode of transportation—the horse and wagon— had proved unreliable. The animals had bolted or been injured or killed. Though desperately needed during the fire, transportation had been hard to find.

Authorities had turned instead to the automobile, commandeering any that they could find. Autos soon proved their usefulness as the speediest message bearers and the most effective mode of transportation available in the stricken city. They served to carry supplies, evacuate the injured, and transport dynamite. After the disaster many eyewitnesses commented on the surprising role the much maligned machines had played in overcoming difficulties caused by the earthquake and fire. Louise Wall, who spent much of the fire exploring the devastated city on foot, wrote of the new role of the automobile:

> [All] private cars had been impressed for public service, some to carry the sick and dying from the burning Mechanics' Pavilion, where the victims of the earth-

quake had been at first taken for safety, and many [to carry] dynamite from Fort Mason to the dynamiters on the fire-line. These gallant little toys of the rich ran almost into the fire, rocking and tottering over the wreckage of the street with their perilous loads of dynamite, and back again to safety. They were the only effective means of locomotion left in the city, where every street car was paralyzed. The automobile is the unquestioned hero of the San Francisco fire.

To address the problem of lost emergency communications, two manual telephone switchboards were purchased around 1913 as part of the police emergency telephone system. The switchboard was installed in the new Hall of Justice. Phones were placed in the homes and offices of city leaders and in fire and police stations for the express purpose of providing communications during disasters. Later renamed the Mayor's Emergency Telephone System, METS would prove useful in the future.

Unfortunately, the most important lessons of the quake—that filled-in ground was unstable and that brick buildings were particularly susceptible to earthquake damage—were ignored. This was due in part to San Francisco's desire to sweep discussion of the earthquake under the civic rug. But most of the blame can be attributed to the city's tremendous haste to rebuild, both to get ready for the Panama–Pacific International Exposition and to make sure that merchants lost as little business as possible. To that end, the Burnham plan was disregarded, and zoning and building-code laws were either weakened or ignored.

Most of the new buildings in the city were actually *more* structurally unsound than their predecessors had been. The one significant improvement to the city skyline

On October 17, 1989, a significant earthquake struck the Bay Area, resulting in extensive damage, including the collapse of sections of the San Francisco Bay Bridge. However, the devastation in the city would not be as severe as that caused by the earthquake of 1906.

was the addition of more steel-frame structures to the downtown area. The steel-frame skyscrapers had proved to be quite resistant to earthquakes, although many "fireproof" ones had been gutted later by the flames. Because the buildings' outer shells had remained intact, however, most were rehabilitated within a few months.

Builders also constructed more nonwood, "fireproof" structures, with built-in standpipes. These pipes, which ran vertically up the entire height of a building, were linked directly to high-pressure water mains. With this feature firefighters would no longer have to pump water up multiple stories, but instead could hook up fire hoses within the building itself.

In spite of San Franciscans' renewed sensitivity to fire, the city allowed contractors to build wooden row houses that lacked fire walls, or fireproof dividers, between units. This gap in the building code would remain for decades, and in the years to come the city would suffer several major multiunit fires.

To clear the city of the extensive mounds of rubble in the streets and on building lots, special rails were laid in the streets. Workers filled railcars with debris and carted it to the bay. In an example of remarkable folly, this rubble was dumped along the bay to fill in the area between Fort Mason and North Beach, where the new Panama–Pacific International Exposition buildings were then constructed. Decades later a fashionable, upper-middle-class district of row homes, called the Marina District, would be built here. The instability of this filled ground would be demonstrated on October 17, 1989.

Late that afternoon, thousands of fans had packed San Francisco's Candlestick Park to await the beginning of the third game of the World Series between northern California rivals the San Francisco Giants and the Oakland A's. Thousands of other Californians were enduring rush-hour traffic on the commute home from work. At 5:04 P.M. the Loma Prieta earthquake struck the Bay Area.

The earthquake was a short, sharp shock measuring 7.1 in magnitude on the Richter scale. The temblor lasted for approximately 15 seconds. Its epicenter was in the Santa Cruz Mountains, near Loma Prieta Mountain, from which the earthquake gets its name. That epicenter was 60 miles south of San Francisco.

The earthquake caused several high-profile disasters. One was the failure of an upper deck of the Bay Bridge, which broke from its moorings on one side and plunged downward onto the lower deck. Remarkably, only one death occurred in the Bay Bridge catastrophe. By far the worst disaster, however, occurred on Oakland's Interstate 880. Forty-four sections of the upper deck of the freeway collapsed, crushing scores of cars

Particularly hard hit during the 1989 quake was the Marina District, a housing development built on the site of the 1915 Panama–Pacific Exposition. The unstable land proved particularly susceptible to the jolt dealt by the 7.1 magnitude earthquake.

underneath their 600-ton weight. The area of the highway that collapsed was built on muddy soil. Local residents of Oakland, from one of the city's poorer districts, immediately responded, risking their lives to help survivors trapped in the wreckage.

The Marina District suffered the worst damage of any area of the city. Several people lost their lives, and hundreds lost their homes and property. During the 15-second tremor the unstable ground beneath the row homes began to liquefy and settle, and the first floors of the homes—which were poorly designed—collapsed. In addition, water and gas mains broke in the liquefied sandy ground, just as they had in many areas in 1906.

Shortly after the quake several gas main explosions

fueled multiple fires in the Marina District. The fires burned out of control for hours until firefighters and citizen volunteers finally managed to contain the flames to a few blocks. Because water main breaks in the South of Market area had drained most of the water supply, firefighters used salt water from the bay to combat the flames. This water was pumped through the fireboat *Phoenix* into the high-pressure water system, just as post-1906 engineers had intended. If San Francisco had not had the foresight to build the auxiliary water system after the 1906 disaster, the city could have suffered the second Great Fire of the century in 1989.

The city's foresight in creating the METS telephone system also paid off. When the 911 telephone system became overloaded with emergency calls, many citizens in need of assistance had to resort to using METS call boxes. Although the switchboard running the emergency system dated from 1913, it functioned smoothly.

The 1989 earthquake dealt San Francisco a harsh blow. The death toll for the Bay Area reached 63. About 28,000 buildings suffered damage—repairs would cost a record $5.9 billion.

Still, the Bay Area was lucky. Compared to the loss of life during the 1906 quake, the death toll was low for a significant earthquake. The Loma Prieta quake's magnitude was fairly high, at 7.1, which is much less than the 7.8 rating of the 1906 quake. The 1989 quake lasted for only 15 seconds, not 45 to 60 seconds as had the 1906 quake. And, perhaps more important, the 1989 quake's epicenter was 60 miles south of San Francisco. In 1906 the epicenter was right near the city.

Many improvements in seismic-resistant building techniques have been made since the 1906 quake—although most took place after the 1971 San Fernando quake in Southern California. That quake caused a scare that led to improved building codes throughout California. It is now unlikely that even a magnitude-8 tremor would cause catastrophic building failure throughout the city.

However, San Francisco and the Bay Area remain quite susceptible to disaster. Until the 1989 quake, city residents had had great confidence in the earthquake-proof claims made by the engineers of their freeway system. However, the extensive damage to Interstate 880 and the Bay Bridge, as well as dangerous cracks that appeared in other roadways, made San Franciscans realize that they are more vulnerable than they had thought.

If the Loma Prieta quake had been as strong, as long, and as close as the 1906 quake, many of San Francisco's roads and bridges would have been devastated. Further liquefaction of unstable soils would have led to a repeat of the disaster to the South of Market area that occurred in 1906. Freeways, such as the Embarcadero Freeway, that sustained enough damage to close for repairs would certainly have collapsed if the shock had been longer and harder.

And there would have been even more devastating fires to contain. The San Francisco Fire Department actually had fewer firefighters in 1989 than it did in 1906—and only one fireboat instead of two. Because firefighters have more-modern equipment today, it is also unlikely that an earthquake-spawned inferno could destroy the entire city. But any earthquake the size of the 1906 quake that takes place in the Bay Area today would become the most costly natural disaster in the history of the United States. The area is now home to more than 6 million people; it is much more densely populated than it was in 1906.

Scientists have found that quakes the size of the 1906 tremor occur once every 200 to 300 years along the San

Andreas Fault. So Bay Area residents may be safe from the "Big One" until the 22nd or 23rd century. But scientists have also found that quakes with a magnitude of 6 or 7 were quite common in the 19th century, leading up to the great earthquake. After 1906 the San Andreas Fault was mostly quiet for more than 60 years. However, after 1979 there were several quakes in the Bay Area: the 1989 Loma Prieta quake was the fourth significant one, and it ruptured the San Andreas in an area that had also ruptured in 1906. This has fueled scientists' concerns that the tension along the San Andreas Fault is growing.

As that tension continues to climb back to pre-1906 levels, Bay Area residents can expect severe shocks to occur with increasing frequency. Local authorities need to uniformly strengthen building codes and outlaw altogether any building on filled soil, and engineers must retrofit or condemn old buildings that don't meet today's tough seismic building codes. San Francisco and its neighboring towns can expect that every major earthquake that hits the region in the future will have the potential to spawn an expensive and deadly disaster.

Chronology

April 18, 1906

5:12 A.M.   Massive earthquake, lasting 45 to 60 seconds and with a magnitude of 7.8, rocks city of San Francisco and surrounding areas; most water mains broken and communications systems destroyed

5:18 A.M.   First aftershock felt, sending panicked citizens back into the streets; approximately 50 fires break out throughout the city

7:45 A.M.   First army troops arrive in San Francisco and receive orders from San Francisco mayor Schmitz to shoot looters

8:14 A.M.   Largest aftershock felt, collapsing some damaged buildings and terrifying residents

10:30 A.M.   Ham and Eggs Fire breaks out in Hayes Valley section of the city

Midday   Most of South of Market area destroyed by fire; evacuation of injured from Mechanic's Pavilion begins

1:00 P.M.   Financial district, behind the Hall of Justice, catches fire; flames threaten Portsmouth Square

2:20 P.M.   Postal telegraph operator transmits last message before being evacuated

2:30 P.M.   Dynamiting of buildings around U.S. Mint at Fifth and Mission Streets begins

3:00 P.M.   Army Signal Corps establishes telegraph operations at Ferry Building; Committee of Fifty meets with Mayor Schmitz

5:00 P.M.   U.S. Mint and Post Office buildings saved from the flames

Evening   Fire breaks out north of Market Street in Delmonico Restaurant; joins with Ham and Eggs Fire and North of Market fire

9:00 P.M.   Firebreak at Powell Street fails to prevent fire from advancing on Nob Hill

April 19, 1906

Early Morning   Fire forces hurried evacuation of refugee camp at Union Square park

2:30 A.M.   St. Francis Hotel at Union Square catches fire; southern end of South of Market fire halted at Townsend Street

Dawn   Nob Hill abandoned to flames; fire moves westward toward Van Ness Avenue; South of Market fire burns into Mission District

Mid-afternoon   Soldiers create firebreak by backfiring and dynamiting eastern side of Van Ness Avenue

Evening   Western side of fire crosses Van Ness Avenue

April 20, 1906

Early morning   Northern side of fire reaches Russian Hill, then advances toward North Beach area

5:00 A.M.   Westward progress of fire halted at Franklin Street; officers and enlisted men from USS *Chicago* supervise rescue of 20,000 refugees from North Beach area

April 21, 1906   Fire in Mission District halted at 20th and Dolores Streets; fire in North Beach is halted at waterfront at Pier 27

May 31, 1906   National Guard withdraws from San Francisco

July 1, 1906   U.S. Army leaves San Francisco

August 1, 1906   Bread lines end

Fall 1906   "Refugee shacks" built for the 11,000 citizens remaining homeless

Spring 1907   Almost all rubble and debris removed from city

1908   Detailed Lawson report on earthquake sets the standard for future earthquake investigations

1915   A rebuilt San Francisco hosts the Panama–Pacific International Exposition

1989   Bay Area shaken by a 7.1 temblor originating south of San Francisco in the Santa Cruz Mountains; extensive damage and severe fires devastate San Francisco's Marina District; 63 Bay Area residents killed

Earthquake and Fire Facts

San Francisco Earthquake of 1906

Date: April 18, 1906

Time: 5:12 A.M.

Magnitude of earthquake: 7.8 (Richter/moment-magnitude scales)

Length of shock: 45 to 60 seconds

Length of rupture on the San Andreas Fault: 280 miles

Average land movement at fault: 12 feet

Maximum land movement at fault: 28 feet

Number of fires reported just after earthquake: 50

Duration of fire: more than 72 hours

Homeless citizens: 225,000

Buildings destroyed: 28,000

Area destroyed: 4.7 square miles; 500 city blocks

Monetary damage: $400 million (1906 dollars)

Dead: Over 3,000

General Earthquake Facts

Longest earthquake ever felt: 4 minutes, Alaska, March 27, 1964 (9.2 magnitude)

Most powerful earthquake ever recorded: 9.5 magnitude, coast of Chile, May 18, 1960

Approximate number of earthquakes per year: 500,000

Approximate number of perceptible earthquakes per year: 100,000

Approximate number of damaging earthquakes per year: 1,000

Most deadly earthquake: eastern Mediterranean region, July 1201. Approximately 1.1 million killed, magnitude unknown

Most deadly 20th-century earthquake: Tangshan, China, July 28, 1976. 242,000 killed, 7.8 in magnitude

Famous Fires

THE GREAT FIRE OF LONDON:

Date: September 2–5, 1666

Cause: Fire in baker's shop spread by powerful winds

Dead: Supposedly 6, most likely much higher

Homeless: 100,000 to 200,000

Damage: Destroyed almost 1 square mile (approximately 4/5 of city), or 13,300 buildings

Positive result: Killed rats carrying the bubonic plague, greatly reducing the toll of the Black Death in subsequent years

THE GREAT CHICAGO FIRE:

Date: October 8–10, 1871

Cause: According to legend, a cow kicked over a lantern in a barn after a long dry spell left the city susceptible to burning

Dead: 250 to 300

Homeless: 90,000 to 100,000

Damage: Destroyed 4 square miles (approximately 1/3 of city), or 17,500 buildings

Positive result: Rebuilding allowed for establishing fire codes and replacing wooden structures with fire-resistant ones

Bibliography

Books and Magazines

Barinaga, Marcia. "Reading the Future in Loma Prieta." *Science,* 27 October 1989, 436–39.

———. "Loma Prieta: Saved by a Short, Sharp Shock." *Science,* 15 December 1989, 1390–91.

Barker, Malcolm E. *Three Fearful Days: San Francisco Memoirs of the 1906 Earthquake and Fire.* San Francisco: Londonborn Publications, 1998.

Bolt, Bruce A. *Earthquakes and Geological Discovery.* New York: Scientific American Library, 1993.

Bronson, William. *The Earth Shook, the Sky Burned.* Garden City, N.Y.: Doubleday & Co., 1959. Reissued in 1997 by Chronicle Books, San Francisco.

Floyd, Candace. *America's Great Disasters.* New York: Mallard Press, 1990.

Fradkin, Philip L. *Magnitude 8: Earthquakes and Life Along the San Andreas Fault.* New York: Henry Holt & Co., 1998.

Hansen, Gladys and Emmet Condon. *Denial of Disaster.* San Francisco: Cameron & Co., 1989.

Kennedy, John Castillo. *The Great Earthquake and Fire: San Francisco, 1906.* New York: William Morrow & Co., 1963.

Levy, Matthys and Mario Salvadori. *Why the Earth Quakes: The Story of Earthquakes and Volcanoes.* New York: W. W. Norton & Co., 1995.

McGraw-Hill Encyclopedia of Science and Technology. 8th ed. Vol 5. New York: McGraw-Hill, 1997.

Magnuson, Ed. *Time.* 30 October 1989, 30–40.

Thomas, Gordon and Max Morgan Witts. *The San Francisco Earthquake.* New York: Stein and Day Publishers, 1971.

Van Rose, Susanna. *Eyewitness Books: Volcano and Earthquake.* New York: Alfred A. Knopf, 1992.

Bibliography

Websites

ABAG (Association of Bay Area Governments)
  Earthquake Maps and Information
www.abag.ca.gov/bayarea/eqmaps/eqmaps.html

Museum of the City of San Francisco
www.sfmuseum.org

National Earthquake Information Center
neic.usqs.gov

Seismolinks
www-socal.wr.usgs.gov/seismolinks.html

Surfing the Internet for Earthquake Data
www.geophys.washington.edu/seismosurfing.html

United States Geological Survey/
  The Great 1906 San Francisco Earthquake
quake.wr.usgs.gov/more/1906/

University of California at Berkeley Seismological Laboratory
www.seismo.berkeley.edu/seismo/

Index

Index

Index

LISA A. CHIPPENDALE is a freelance editor, writer, and violinist. She has worked in a variety of publishing genres, including magazines, scientific journals, books, and children's fiction. She lives outside Philadelphia with her husband, Ross Beauchamp, a freelance cello player and teacher.

JILL McCAFFREY has served for four years as national chairman of the Armed Forces Emergency Services of the American Red Cross. Ms. McCaffrey also serves on the board of directors for Knollwood—the Army Distaff Hall. The former Jill Ann Faulkner, a Massachusetts native, is the wife of Barry R. McCaffrey, a member of President Bill Clinton's cabinet and director of the White House Office of National Drug Control Policy. The McCaffreys are the parents of three grown children: Sean, a major in the U.S. Army; Tara, an intensive care nurse and captain in the National Guard; and Amy, a seventh grade teacher. The McCaffreys also have two grandchildren, Michael and Jack.

Picture Credits